12 STRATEGIES

FOR

SUCCESS

Success is a steady and consistent progress towards your

personal and professional goals as designed by you

Jim Rohn

12 STRATEGIES

FOR

SUCCESS

Ordinary people achieving extraordinary results
By applying these simple success strategies

DR. M. JOSHUA-AMADI

DEDICATION

With profound gratitude and deep appreciation,
I dedicate this book to my mentor and benefactor

Stanley Lewis Rodway

Who shared his wisdom, lived experience and
epiphanies with me in the very short time I was
privileged to know him.
Thank you

ACKNOWLEDGEMENT

I wish to acknowledge my Supreme Mentor, Encourager, Teacher, Motivator, wonderful Counsellor and Inspirer. With You all things become possible. Without You I can do nothing. Your daily light, help and guidance are gratefully appreciated.

I wish to acknowledge my dear parents, Huldah and Joshua Amadi, without whom I may never have aspired to anything. You encouraged me when no one else did and spurred me on to where I am today. Your loving kindness was the foundation of my being. You gave me a wonderful start in life and values that nurtured my self-esteem. You taught me to believe in myself as a springboard for ambition and courage for action. Thank you for the harvest of your teaching and your lives.

My teachers Edna Whitehouse and William Wray, thank you for your words of wisdom that motivated and encouraged me to act and apply your teachings to ensure my success.

To you the reader, without you none of this would happen. Thank you for your continued support and patronage. May the insights from this book make a profound difference as you read and apply them in your personal and professional life.

Finally to God be all the glory for His enduring grace and kindness through the years.

CONTENTS

PREFACE

This book evolved out of my lived experience. After struggling through life and succeeding in many areas, I decided to share what I have learned over time in order to help others succeed in their journey. The book is also informed and enriched by decades of studying the lives and times of highly successful people and by researching and observing living millionaires and billionaires over time. As I have received and am still receiving, I have distilled the techniques and testimonies from these studies, into twelve simple but powerful keys for success.

I have labelled them strategies, meaning plans to get you from where you are to where you want to be. They are also tools in your toolkit of life. You can select those you need to apply to your life and use them to achieve success and happiness.

The greatest quest in life is for financial success and happiness. Many people just want to be happy. Some want to succeed and be free from money worries to live the life of their dreams.

Unfortunately many have not succeeded in finding success with money or the elusive happiness they seek and have become discouraged.

However, success in any area of life is no longer a secret. Successful people have opened the door of the citadel to knowledge, information and strategies for success in any area. Therefore anyone can now succeed in their relationships, careers, jobs, finances, health and fitness, emotional balance, spiritual and mental harmony. Thus, anyone can find happiness to live the life they desire and deserve.

There are many books on success and happiness in the market. However, this book is based on two decades of research and diligent application that yielded and continues to produce immense results in every area of my life. It is a self-help book and a book of discovery. In it you will discover the areas you need to discipline yourself or work harder in order to achieve the success you seek and find happiness.

The twelve strategies for success range from desire and dreams you have for your life, to purpose that gives direction and meaning to your quest. There is a laser sharp focus to concentrate the mind and actions to achieve your objective.

You will also learn the importance of forming success habits through discipline, hard work and going the extra mile. Service offers you the opportunity to get what you want by helping others get what they want. Commitment to excellence ensures you are the best in your area of competence and gives you back your personal power.

The book rounds off with having a positive mental attitude which accounts for 80% of success. As Denis Waitley said, "The winner's edge is all in the attitude. Attitude is the criterion for success." Successful people have applied these same strategies over time to remain at the top of their game, living a balanced and harmonious life of abundance and happiness. By emulating their diligence and discipline, you too can succeed in your personal and professional life and be happy to live the life of your dreams.

A chapter on the power duo of gratitude and forgiveness has been added as the icing on the cake or the baker's dozen on the journey of success. Those who heed the hint and apply them will succeed faster and easier than those who do not.

There are exercises at the end of each chapter to help you measure and monitor your progress and adjust your plans and steps towards the success you desire.

I have applied these strategies to my life and used them as success keys to open doors and watched them produce profound and lasting results over time. They have greatly enriched my life and enabled me to live the life of my dreams. It is my ardent hope that they too would enrich your personal and professional life with the success and happiness you seek as you study, understand and diligently apply them.

Many of life's failures are people who did not realize how close they were to success when they gave up trying

Thomas Edison

INTRODUCTION

Success is following and realising your deepest dreams
and desires by achieving your goals with
the zeal of a two-year-old child

Everyone wants to succeed in life and be happy. Many people struggle to succeed in their personal and professional lives and be free from frustrating worries and anxiety. Unfortunately many do not manage to find the success they deserve either in their personal or professional lives. Consequently, they resign themselves to accepting and tolerating whatever life dishes out to them. Many are unhappy.

Some have struggled until they became discouraged and decided that they were not good enough or don't deserve success. So they settled for less than they deserve. Some of these unfortunate people have concluded that success is far-fetched and not for the likes of them. Some think that success still has secrets and mysteries only a few are privileged to understand and know. Nothing could be further from the truth.

Most success secrets are now in the public domain. Successful millionaires and billionaires have let us behind the scenes to look in, understand and know the once accepted secrets of success and even to apply them to our own lives and succeed.

Therefore, sceptics have no more room for argument or doubt that anyone who diligently desires success can achieve it by applying the strategies that make for success. However, some people are still held hostage by their negative mindset. As King Solomon said, "As a man thinks in his heart so is he," (Proverbs 23:7). So as you think in your mind and believe in your heart, so you become.

Bondage of Negativity

Some people are held hostage by their negative thoughts and limiting beliefs about success. Consequently, they sabotage their own effort by their thoughts and beliefs and remain sad, unsuccessful and limited from what they could have. Meanwhile those who change their thoughts to fit and align with prevailing findings are liberated from these self-limiting beliefs and destructive negative thoughts. Perhaps you can identify with some of these...

Here's the challenge

Maybe you are one of these unfortunate people.

Over the years you've got used to settling for less and you heard people tell you that you can't do this and you can't do that. Maybe they said you're not smart enough or clever enough to succeed. Or maybe you tried to accomplish something and it didn't work out the way you wanted - so you thought: "Maybe I don't know how enough..."

"Maybe they are right, I just can't find success." Then you gave up and settled for less... You believed a lie.

You accepted those limiting beliefs. You accepted the negative thoughts that you can't ever find or have success in life.

But today you can get what you want in life.
You don't have to settle for less any more.
When you settle for less you feel less than and become less.
Your dreams die.
Your shoulders sag.
You become frustrated with life and people.

Why?

Because when you think you're not good enough, or you think and believe that you cannot succeed, you attract and create more pain, more struggle, more hardship and life gets harder and harder.

That's because what you think and believe is what you create. You get in life, what you are willing to tolerate and accept and not what you want. You also get in life what you are prepared for and hence deserve and not what you want.

Here's where it gets interesting…But you want more from life and you want to make more money. You want to get a better job. You want to spend more time with your family, and you want to achieve those goals and live your dream. You want to lose that weight. You want to get in shape and look good and feel good about yourself?

You want to enjoy your life and have more fun and you want better health. You want a better and happy life... and you can have exactly what you want.

How?

You have to get rid of that negative thinking that others gave you. You get rid of those negative limiting beliefs which aren't really true...

Today, you can turn things around and you can stop settling for less. Today, you can get what you want and deserve.
Today, you can find success in any area of your life.
You can achieve your goals, and you can enjoy your life and have fun. You can make more money.

You can be happy now and you can get that great job you desire. You can meet the right person and enjoy a nurturing and fulfilling relationship. You can also be healthier and get in shape. You can stop settling for less because now, you'll put an end to the struggle, the pain and the frustrations.

By applying these simple but powerful strategies in this book, you will ensure that you'll find success and happiness in both your personal and professional life. Yes others have achieved it sometimes effortlessly but often with resolute determination and hard work. But it is doable and it is possible. It is proven. So why can't you?

Today, I encourage you to read and study these 12 Strategies for Success with an open mind and apply them in any area of your life where you desire success and what worked for countless others will also work for you. Believe that it can and it would. As Brian Tracy said, "Life is like a combination lock; your job is to find the right numbers, in the right order, so you can have anything you want." In this book you'll also find several success testimonies from those who have applied these strategies in their own life and made it to live the lifestyle they only dreamed of not long ago. It is my ardent hope that you too would study what has worked for them and apply it to your own life for an enduring life of success and happiness.

CHAPTER 1

What is Success?

Success is the progressive realisation of a worthy goal or ideal
Earl Nightingale

Success is to be measured not so much by the position that one has reached in life as by the obstacles which he has overcome while trying to succeed
Booker T. Washington

Success is the sum of small efforts repeated everyday, day in and day out
Robert Collier

These three great and successful men capture and epitomise my idea of success through struggle, pain, countless obstacles and challenges but daily progressing to achieve and realise a worthy goal. Often there is nothing to hang unto but hope and faith but through relentless persistence, we make it to shore against all the opinions and expectations of critics, the Nay Sayers and sometimes, well-meaning protectors!

From our definition of success, you can succeed as a home-maker or a rainmaker. You can succeed as a judge or janitor. You can succeed as a chief executive or the captain of industry. You can succeed in raising children or raising chicken. Many have succeeded as bakers and bankers, tradesmen and tailors, salesperson and sailors. Whatever your desire and goal, you can succeed in it and live to enjoy your dream.

Success is relative. As you move progressively from where you are to where you want to be in a steady consistent manner until you get there, you are succeeding.

The trappings of success many see on the outside are the external manifestations or reflection of inner success. Success is an inside job. You can succeed even when there is nothing to show for it. You can succeed financially without a penny to your name but if your attitude is right and you keep on keeping on, the visible evidence of your success will surely follow to reflect your inner success.

However, you cannot succeed on the outside until you succeed within. Even if you succeed through financial winnings, without the expansion of your consciousness to receive and accommodate wealth and riches, you will lose all and fall back to your original state before winning. Some lottery winners are potent examples of this. Many do fall back to their financial positions prior to winning and some may become destitute.

Thus, the importance of success is not the position attained or the outward trappings but in the valuable person you are becoming in the process of trying to succeed. As General

Douglas MacArthur said, "Life is a lively process of really becoming."

Therefore do not disdain or complain about your struggles and hardships on your way to Success Street. Rejoice. You are becoming the person you were created to be. Hardship, hard work and adversity can only strengthen your success muscle, making you more resilient and wiser as you grow valuable as a person.

Today, decide to make every day and every week a success. This will make your year a success and soon your life will be transformed and become successful, as you progress towards your worthy goal or ideal with enthusiasm, passion and energy.

What is Strategy?

The dictionary defines strategy as a plan, procedure or policy. It is a step by step approach to get you from where you are to where you want to be. It is a guide or road map for directions unto your desired destination. With a success plan all you need is its diligent application and you can get to where you desire to be. The steps for your goal attainment are provided (in Chapter 2).

There is now no excuse for not applying these simple strategies for success and being happy. As Albert Einstein said, "You have to learn the rules of the game and then you have to play better than anyone else." You have the rules of success for your happiness. Now go and play better than your past self and succeed.

What is Happiness?

Jim Rohn writes, "Happiness is a life well-lived and filled with people of substance, a wide variety of experiences and memories that become priceless forms of currency to use, spend and invest." Happiness is a universal quest and results from the joy of activity, achievement and accomplishment. It is a practice of living in the now.

Happiness is also a skill acquired through experience and awareness that feeds the enjoyment of life with contentment, whatever the prevailing situation or circumstance.

It is learning to set your life sails to make every wind favourably disposed to getting you to your desired destination or haven. It is the preserve of those who would fully expand their experience, consciousness and horizons to learn without judgment and attain mastery over their passions, emotions and prevailing circumstances.

Happiness is the ability to handle disappointments, rejections and defeats without losing your enthusiasm or sense of well-being. It is in living a harmonious lifestyle.

Happiness is a mental attitude to be content, a by-product of accomplishment from action leading to self-fulfilment. It is a continuation of happenings not resisted and gratitude for those misfortunes avoided. It is a choice or decision made that forms a habit.

Happiness is like the light of a candle. It can light a thousand others without being diminished. It is shared and enjoyed by many yet remains. It is more in being and not in having.

It is freedom from negative emotions of fear, worry, greed, jealous envy and bitter resentment, the little foxes that ruin the vine and pollute personality. It is a way of interpreting the world and its events with detachment while remaining whole.

Why seek happiness?

Happiness is discussed alongside success because many people think and say "If only I can succeed at so and so then I will be happy." This is a myth. It is to dispel this happiness-success myth that it is discussed here. You can be happy right now.

Happiness is a decision and a choice. If you want you can decide and choose it now. There is no reason to wait until you attain a goal to be happy. You can be happy on your way to achieving your goal.

As you progressively achieve goals, you'll become happier and more ecstatic when you attain the ultimate goal of your dreams. Thus, the choice or decision of happiness is a potent motivator. It inspires you with the zeal and energy to pursue and attain your goals and so increase your level of happiness.

However, without deciding to choose to be happy now, you will remain discouraged waiting for happiness to show up before you take action. Meanwhile happiness waits for you to choose it and get to work. Today, choose to be happy and let it inspire and motivate you into action, free from despondency, inertia and procrastination.

For happiness is not an elusive feeling. Like success, it is an enduring habit acquired through self-discipline and the willingness to practice until it becomes ingrained.

What is discipline?

George Washington wrote, "Discipline is the soul of an army. It makes small numbers formidable; procures success to the weak and esteem to all." This great man's observation has not lost its value or importance today. If the army can rely on simple discipline to procure success and esteem for happiness, why can't individuals use the same strategy to obtain the success and happiness they desire?

Mike Ditka said, "Success is not measured by money, power or social rank. Success is measured by discipline." By applying self-discipline to cut out anything that holds you back from success and building success habits you succeed to become happier. Thus, success and happiness are available as by-products of self-discipline and the willingness to work hard and practice until success habits become ingrained.

When discipline is firmly established as a habit, it becomes a formidable opponent to fear of failure or defeat and the fickle discouragement when goals are not achieved and other negative emotions the human heart feels. We must suffer one or two things writes, Jim Rohn, "The pain of discipline or the pain of regret and disappointment." Life is full of choices and each of us must bear the consequences of our choices.

Discipline is the foundation for success. Without it failure is certain but with it, you can achieve success. It enables you to do the things you don't want or like to do. It forces you to take action even when you don't feel like it. That's what all successful people do daily that makes and keeps them successful. You can do the same and succeed. Discipline renders a death blow to the thief of life called procrastination.

Athletes and sports people understand and treasure the power of discipline. That's what makes and keeps them as winners. The same discipline in your personal and professional life can make you a success, living the life you dream of with serenity.

Discipline is a master key to success. It unlocks the doors to wealth of any kind, material, spiritual, financial, emotional, mental and relational unto abundance. It opens the floodgates of activity for accomplishment, self-actualisation, happiness, pride of achievement and satisfaction to boost flagging self-esteem and enhance self-confidence.

However, to achieve discipline requires self-analysis on where you need it, and the willingness to commit and persevere with it until goal is attained. The rewards of discipline far outweigh the momentary discomfort of acquiring the habit. Thus, the keys to success and happiness you seek are readily available through self-discipline.

Exercise to chapter 1

What is your definition of success?

What is your experience trying to succeed?

How do you rate your success level from 1-10 in these areas?

(1 being the least successful and 10 being the most)

- Physically
- Mentally
- Relationally
- Emotionally
- Financially
- Spiritually
- Socially
- Professionally (career)

What are your personal and professional goals?

What can you do now to enhance your success in these areas?

What action can you take today to move you towards achieving your worthy goal?

CHAPTER 2

Desire

A strong, deeply seated desire is the beginning of all human achievement, not hope, not a wish, but a keen pulsating desire which transcends everything. It is the seed from which all human accomplishment spring

Napoleon Hill

Desire is the will to win that goes beyond aspiration and hankering. It is a resolute determination to win whatever it takes. It trumps talent, skill and education. Desire is an idea, a thought or deep longing either to do or to have, that cannot be quenched.

Nothing can stop the man or woman who desires to achieve. Obstacles, challenges and hindrances are mere hurdles to overcome. They strengthen your muscles and make you even more determined. With desire, all you need is a goal and a plan. (Plans and steps for goal achievement are provided at the end of this chapter).

For example, the steel magnate, Andrew Carnegie said, "First I knew that I wanted to go into making steel. I whipped up that desire until it became a driving obsession with me. By this I mean that my desire drove me day and night. Then I took the next step." Desire energises you to take the next step and to keep taking action until you achieve your goal. For to desire is to obtain and to aspire is to achieve. However, without the requisite action, desire becomes only a wishful thinking.

A burning desire is what it takes to achieve success in any area. Desire gives you a reason to get up everyday and relentlessly pursue your goal. It galvanises you with the staying power to pick yourself up after each setback, disappointment or disaster and start all over again without excuse, blame or complaint. Without a burning, red hot desire, you will quit at the first sign of challenge, adversity or obstacle. Why?

Because the mountain slopes of success are strewn with the bones of those who started off very eager to succeed. Along the way when things got tough, they settled down to rest a while and in resting they perished without reaching their goal or destination.

Quitting in the face of hardship and suffering is a natural human behaviour. Most people take the line of least resistance. They quit and find excuses to justify their lack of resilience and discipline to stay the course. That's why many fail to succeed.

But successful people endure and even cherish hardship and keep setting higher and more daring goals. As Mohammad Ali said, "What keeps me going is goals." Thus, they keep moving forward and achieving more daring goals with enthusiasm.

Testimony

A young man, here called Jack, wrote a book about how anyone can make money in real estate without any money down. A reporter called him a fraud and dared him to prove his plan. Jack went to the local Job Centre and gave fliers to three hundred unemployed men and women, supposedly looking for work. He invited them to three days of lectures to teach them his plan and to help them to make money. Only fifty (17%), showed up for his classes. When Jack explained the amount of work needed to make the plan work, forty five of the fifty left, remaining only five people (2%).

After their first gruelling day of finding properties for sale, another three quit leaving only a couple. This couple persevered and made five thousand dollars in three days. They helped Jack to prove his plan and get the sceptic reporter off his case.

Please note that out of a total of three hundred unemployed people at the Job Centre only one couple made it (0.7%) or one person in the original fifty that showed up (2%). Similar studies show that only 2-5% of the population dare to succeed even though many say and claim that they seek success, especially financial success.

Desire is also ambition, aspiration or the yearning for accomplishment. It starts off as an idea that often comes with its own positive energy and enthusiasm that drives you to begin, then progress and gain the momentum needed along the way to execution and completion. Desire demands total commitment and firm resolution to stay the course like an endurance race without quitting. Can you commit to endure hardship and win?

Why do you desire success? Deep seated desire can motivate and galvanise you into action more than anything else and keep you taking necessary action until you succeed. Successful people are often motivated by these ten desires:

- The pride and joy of achievement
- Financial gain as security against worries and fear of lack
- To gain public acclaim (reputation)
- To be recognised as successful
- To use innate abilities and talents for self-expression
- Self-preservation
- Gain freedom from dependent position
- Leave a worthy legacy
- Anger, usually due to envy or to prove something
- Fear of being seen as a failure or being overtaken by others

Whatever your motive for desiring success, it must be important and strong enough to inspire you to take the initiative for action. Successful people are always people of action. They know that without requisite action, desires die and nothing is achieved.

Unfortunately, some people are driven by force of necessity to seek success through financial gain. They don't often get very far when they meet with challenges and hardship along the way. But those propelled by a burning desire, turned into the obsession to achieve and are motivated by any of the above factors, often succeed in their quest. As Napoleon Hill said, "Nothing great is ever achieved without a definite motive."

Desire is a major key for your success and connects you to the success you desire. Today, you can expect to succeed and you surely will. No one but you can desire success for you. Not your parent, spouse, friend or foe. Why? Your own resolution to win and the will to succeed are more important than anyone's opinion or view.

Exercise to chapter 2

What do you desire today?

- Is it financial freedom to spend your time as you wish?
- A nurturing relationship?
- To start a business and make more money?
- Promotion from your job?
- Personal recognition or accomplishment?
- Social acceptance and status?
- Freedom from fear and self-doubt?
- More self-confidence and personal power?
- Better health and looking good?
- More fun in your life to live your dream?
- Family restoration, reunion and unity?

Whatever your desire, plan it out today and set it out as a goal. Goals allow you to control the direction of change in your favour. Drive your desire to a red hot burning obsession like Andrew Carnegie did and you too can succeed as he did.

Here's a six point plan to help you achieve your goal

1. You must have a specific clear goal. Like exactly how much money you want.
    Work out the exact amount you need to end the money worries and anxiety

2. You must have a specific time frame in which to achieve it, like in one month or a year
    Setting a timeframe makes it mandatory for you to go after it with gusto.

3. You must write it down clearly and set it where you can see it everyday as a reminder. There is something about written down goals that set them apart. People with clear written goals accomplish far more in shorter time frames than those without. Your power of daily visualisation will enhance goal attainment.

4. You must have a step by step daily plan of action of how to achieve your goal. Each step should move you closer to your dream. Without a daily to-do list, it will all seem overwhelming. So chunk it down to bite sizes and start now. You may have to adjust it along the way but start.

5. You must pay the price. What will you give up or acquire to make it happen? Is it money or leisure time or energy?
    You must give up something of value or acquire better skills to achieve it.

Then you must take immediate, repeated, massive action daily to achieve it.

6. From now on you must think about reaching your goals everyday to make it happen. Whatever you consistently think about, you will empower to bring about.

So go for gold today. Persevere to achieve your goal. You deserve great success.

CHAPTER 3

Dream Big

The future belongs to those who believe in the beauty of their dreams

Eleanor Roosevelt

Big dreamers are the architects and saviours of the world. Prophets, poets, sages, sculptors, composers and architects, dreamed lofty dreams to change the landscape.

Without a big dream you are like a dead person. All successful people are big dreamers. They are like children. They let their imagination run wild, soar and roam to dream big without any concern of how the dream will be accomplished. The Universe will see to that.

Their burning desire to succeed gives wings to their imagination to dream gigantic big dreams. Without big dreams there is nothing to stretch your imagination to create anything. As Mohammad Ali said, "The man who has no imagination has no wings." Big dreams empower and energise us with innovative ideas and insight for creativity.

Dream is the inspiration for winning. It is the fire that ignites your desire and drives you into action to achieve. Without a lofty dream, what does desire have to work on?

With a giant dream out of proportion to your own human ability you must enlist the help of divine forces to aid its accomplishment. Such are the dreams that bring great resounding memorable success that endure through time. Imagine if Michelangelo only had an ordinary dream for painting the ceiling of the Sistine Chapel in Rome.

Big gigantic dreams are ideas and visions of where you are going. They force you to develop your potentials to achieve them. They encourage you to take massive action and expend energy to attain them. They enlighten you to possibilities, opportunities and ways available to fulfil them. Many people want to live the life of their dreams. It is their driving force every waking day that keeps them hungry and thirsty for life. For as you dream so shall you become. Dreams are the seedlings that become realities.

Many follow their big dreams and find self-fulfilment along the way. The importance of dreams is their ability to force us to grow, develop and mature into the valuable person we become while trying to succeed. The value is in the path and process and not in the attainment. Thus, a big dream is a potent driving force giving us the will to win and birthing total self-belief. This is because, if you can believe it, smell it, taste it and feel it, you can have it, for it surely will happen.

Many successful people get a buzz chasing their dreams. The thrill of the chase is more rewarding than achieving the goal. Some successful people dream of financial goals and most have lifestyle dreams to improve their quality of life or a combination of both. The younger the dreamer, the more the dreams are money-based. The older ones have quality of life dreams. Whatever your age, today, dream the big dreams.

However, if you have no dreams what are you living for? What drives your life to get up daily to do anything? If you have no dreams forcing you to act, life will act on you by default. If you have no dreams to live for, people will enrol you into their agenda.

If you have no dreams to focus and direct your life, activities and energy how can you manifest the greatness within you? How can you utilise all your wonderful gifts, talents and abilities? How can you challenge yourself to create anything? Remember King Solomon said, "Without vision, the people perish." So get a big dream to die for.

Unfortunately, many people dream small, minute dreams they can handle and set their sights so low that they achieve it in no time and fizzle out. Then they settle for the status quo and begin on the slippery slope to decline. Many die slowly and regrettably with their big dreams still within them. What is your dream today?

Let others dream small dreams to live small lives but not you. Let others argue over small petty things but not you. Let others cry over small inconsequential slights and hurts but not you. Let others aspire and hope without taking action but not you. But let your dreams be so big that in achieving them as goals, you become something worth becoming. Dreaming small leaves you tackling meaningless things to achieve mediocrity. But with giant dreams, small things get taken care of along the way.

Big dreamers leave us a worthy memorable legacy. Though they fade away like old soldiers, their lives and dreams still speak. For example, Abraham Lincoln had a dream to get to the White House and settle the slavery issue in America. It took him thirty long years to get there but he succeeded and in four years he settled it.

Nelson Mandela had a dream to rescue apartheid South Africa from racial hatred and segregation. It took him thirty four years through harsh imprisonment at the notorious Robben Island to do so but he succeeded. And said, "The sun never set on such a glorious achievement." He was rewarded with being the first black President of a free South Africa. As Henry David Thoreau said, "If one advances confidently in the direction of his dreams and endeavours to live the life which he has imagined, he will meet with success unexpected in common hours." These two men succeeded.

Martin Luther King junior had the mother of all dreams. He dreamed of when people in America will no longer be judged by the colour of their skin but by the content of their character. He made his famous speech to plant the seed of his dream in 1963.

Exactly forty five years later to the day, a young African American got a ticket to the White House. President Barack

Obama was barely two years old when the seed of King's dream was sown at Lincoln Memorial in Washington. But today, he is a living epitome of that dream. You may not live to see your dreams manifested and realised as Martin Luther King junior did not, but someone somewhere will run with it and fulfil it.

Personal Testimony

A certain lady also had a dream. As a young mother, she was forced to marry as a teenager according to the custom and traditions of men in her generation. She wanted to go to school and study but she was not allowed to. Instead she married and had children. She did the next best thing. She had a dream that all her children would be graduates. No one in her lineage had ever gone to school. She only spent three years at the local school learning to read and write. How is it possible for her children to go to college let alone graduate?

She did not know how but she had a dream. She had no money to send them to college but she had a dream. She had no social connections to help her get them there. But she had a dream. She agonised until she remembered that she also had a God who helps the helpless in hopeless situations. She knew that she could call on a God who never fails. She had nothing but she knew how to pray. So she got on her knees and she prayed. She prayed tirelessly through the nights and prayed joyfully and gratefully through the days.

Prayer became her obsession because she wanted all her children to be educated and earn their degrees as graduates. They must transcend the lack of education in her lineage. Her burning desire for education must be accomplished in her children.

She prayed as only a mother could pray. And the Lord of glory heard her prayers as He heard that of Hannah, Rachel and countless other mothers before her. He granted her favour for her request and guided all her children through education.

Today, all her children are graduates. She succeeded in her desire and dream and lived to see them all graduate and reward her diligence in prayer. That lady my friend, was my mother, Huldah. I am a product of her earnest prayers and evidence of God's grace, favour and faithfulness to helpless and needy people in hopeless situations.

You may not have a gigantic dream to rescue a nation from racial segregation or to change the course of history by abolishing slavery and racial bigotry and hatred but you can dream like my mother to change your family heritage and situation. You can also change your life and circumstance by dreaming big and achieving your dreams.

Importance of dreams

Dreams are really baits or enticement to get you to commit to personal growth and development so you can be more and reveal your true greatness. Without such a lofty dream you cannot challenge, stretch and develop your abilities, talents and gifts to pursue and attain your vision and live your dreams. You cannot reach your goals and manifest the true greatness within you. But your dream is not your destiny.

Destiny is a much bigger picture than a dream. The pursuit of your dream leads you along the path to fulfil your destiny and manifest your greatness within.

Destiny is what God has fashioned for you and only He knows the magnitude and extent of it and how it would be crafted and used to manifest your true greatness. It is so great that if He told you about it, your finite mind cannot comprehend it and the magnitude of it may overwhelm you.

For example, Nelson Mandela had a dream to rid his homeland of social injustice and racial segregation called apartheid. When apartheid was dismantled Nelson Mandela had his dream. But his destiny was not yet manifested. He was to be the first black President of a free South Africa. At the beginning of the struggle, if he had been told that he would one day become a president in South Africa, it would have staggered his young mind and may have changed the course of history. But by pursuing his dream he reached his destiny.

Biblical Joseph also had a dream that his jealous brothers will one day bow down to him. When they came to buy food in Egypt, they inadvertently bowed down to him as the Prince of Egypt, without whom no one could buy or sell in Egypt. Joseph was living his dream life right there in Egypt. But God who gave him the dream also had a destiny for Joseph, a bigger more encompassing vision of greatness to unfold.

After their father prophesied over them and died, Joseph realised the magnitude of his dream and its significance in the birthing of the nation of Israel. From the birth of a nation, Joseph's greatness unfolded even more to include the birth of the Messiah, the Saviour of the world. Now, had God told a young seventeen year old Joseph that through his simple obedience to a dream, the rest of humanity would be saved, it would have been too much for his young mind. Perhaps his jealous brothers would have really killed him, to end his dream to reign over them. Thus, dreams are the beginning of a greater vision that unfolds along your journey of life into destiny.

More importantly, the dreams allow you to grow, develop your talents, acquire skills, discover your strength and hone your abilities until you are mentally and emotionally prepared and ready with a noble resilient character in alignment with your vision. You see, Joseph had to go from the pits to Potiphar's house and serve as a slave. There he lived to learn the life of slavery in Egypt. He also learnt Egyptian custom and lifestyle. He had to be incarcerated in prison to meet and learn palace protocol from Pharaoh's baker and cupbearer.

These trials were for his personal development along the path of his destiny. Thus, his dream led him on his destined path to prepare him for his true life mission, from which his greatness was manifested.

Today, let your dreams lead you to personal and professional growth, development and maturity. Expand your consciousness to receive the fruits of your dream. Let the person you are becoming line up and align with the vision of your inner greatness.

Personal Testimony

Personally I wanted to be a medical doctor to help my people when there were no doctors within a ten mile radius. Many died on the way to the hospital and some did not even bother to attempt the journey. That was the need and dream that inspired and motivated me. Having achieved my dream and worked for twenty years, I was called away to go and teach. I was still not sure of what I was supposed to teach. But as I travelled along my path, the vision began to unfold. I started to develop myself and acquire requisite skills and knowledge.

Today, I write, research, teach and help others improve their attitude so they can succeed in their personal and professional lives and make more money. I would never have seen or understood the wider vision as a youngster or aspiring medical student. This is the power of big dreams. They lead you along your destined path to develop and equip you for a greater mission.

Today, I challenge you to dream big. By tackling big dreams, smaller ones take care of themselves along the way. Don't die with your dream still within you. You owe it to yourself and to humanity to succeed, achieve your dreams and live your destiny.

14 Qualities of Dreams

- Your dream is birth within you often from your life's tragedies, trials or traumas
- Your dream determines the people chosen to surround you
- Your dream may require a geographical relocation

- Your dream should be the object of your intense focus
- Your dream should dictate who you allow access to you (dream killers or nurturers?)
- Your dream requires periods of preparation
- Neglect of your dream ensures its demise
- Your dream may be misunderstood by some people around you
- The magnitude of your dream may intimidate and daunt you
- Your dream is progressively revealed and enlarged as you pursue it
- Passion for your dream must be sufficient for its attainment without external encouragement
- Your dream may expose you to resentment and anger from others
- Every relationship should either move you towards or away from your dream
- Relentless pursuit of your dream is the evidence of your desire to achieve it

Exercise to chapter 3

- How great is your personal dream?
- How big is your professional dream?
- How can you let your dreams soar on the wings of your imagination?
- Great things result from great dreams. How can you dream bigger dreams?
- How can you overcome your fears and self-doubt to dreaming big?
- What mental limits have you placed on your vision for your future?
- Can you let your need and desperation inspire you to loftier dreams?
- How would you like to be remembered? Big dreams can birth and turn ordinary lives into extra-ordinary legacies.

CHAPTER 4

Clear Sense of Direction

He who has a why to live, can bear almost any how

Friedrich Nietzsche

You must have a crystal clear reason why you want to succeed and in what areas you seek success. Without this clarity you cannot sustain the effort needed to pursue and attain success. Clarity of purpose and the specificity of what you want provide a direction and road map to your quest for success. If you don't know where you are going and why you are going, why bother? A clear sense of direction is needed to channel your effort and resources for speedier attainment of the success you seek.

Successful people develop a clear sense of direction. They envision and imagine what their lives would be like at their chosen destination and then work backwards crafting the necessary steps to get them there. They work daily on their goals until achieved. They also have a crystal clear idea of where they are now, where they want to go in a specific time frame and why they desire to get there. Everyday they know precisely what they scheduled to do to move them closer to their destination. They are experts at avoiding all forms of distraction, diversions and interruptions from their set goals.

These are the habits that make them successful. They just have successful habits.

Unfortunately, unsuccessful people have no such clarity with where they are now, where they want to go or any plans about their tomorrow. They either drift with the current and get washed ashore on some strange island or get distracted and wonder how they got there. Either way they are adrift, often rootless and purposeless. Some become easy prey to petty worry, anxiety or fear, leading to failure and unhappiness.

Successful people know exactly what their destination looks like, feels like, tastes like and smells like. They live there in their imagination and often assume the feeling of having realised their desire. Consequently, their success is often not delayed.

Successful people also have the rare ability to endure any situation that confronts them and continue taking meaningful and necessary action in the direction of their goals. Because they know where they are going and why, they can take challenges in their stride and overcome them. Ultimately they succeed. Nothing can stop them.

Unsuccessful people are busy blaming others for their plight and complaining about their circumstances. Instead of taking full and total responsibility for their lives and actions, they prefer to shift the blame to anyone including dead parents, siblings, the government, economy, the taxman and their foes.

Until you take total responsibility for your life and your mistakes in life, you are not in control and success will elude you. Today, model and imitate successful people and take full responsibility for your life and situation. What you don't acknowledge and own, you cannot change. Taking responsibility is what gives you that personal power over your circumstances, events and situations you encounter and enables you to triumph over them and succeed.

Successful people are clear about their expected outcome. They are very result and action-oriented. They are expectant of favourable outcomes. They consistently and continuously take action in the direction of their clear and concise goals and objectives. With a clear sense of direction, clarity of purpose and focused concentration, they become virtually unstoppable. You too can succeed by following their example.

Exercise to chapter 4

- Do you have a clear direction of your objectives?
- What is the destination of your dreams and desire?
- What is your life purpose?
- If not yet discovered are you searching for it?
- If discovered are you pursuing it?
- How clear and concise is the vision of your dream life?

CHAPTER 5

Focus

But one thing I do: Forgetting those things which are behind and reaching forward to those things which are ahead, I press towards the goal for the prize of the upward call of God in Christ Jesus.

Paul of Tarsus (Philippians 3:13-14)

Focus is a fixed point where you concentrate your energy, attention and resources. When you concentrate your time and effort hitting the same target of your interest and desire, you will succeed in beating it into submission. Great sports women and men, athletes, musicians and dancers know the power of focused concentration and practice.

They put in the time and effort needed again and again and through painful and tireless practicing, they progress to perform as brilliantly as we see them. They become successful at tournaments. Thus, by practice, focusing on their strength, ability, desire, calling or mission they become proficient and perform to success.

Paul of Tarsus sacrificed his family and the comforts of a married home life to pursue his one desire and mission in life. He knew there was a pressing-in to attain the goal. He shunned all distraction, detours and diversions to succeed in achieving more than any other preacher before or after him.

He wrote two thirds of the New Testament that has encouraged, inspired, comforted, motivated and taught millions of people world-wide. That is the power of focus. It aids success in any area of endeavour.

But to succeed in life you must finish your past and lay all the ghosts to rest and move on with your life. This important key to success rests on focusing the conscious mind on the things that you desire and dream of achieving rather than your past failing, people's opinions and views and what your parents did or failed to do. As an adult you must take total responsibility for your life and craft a self-image that's worthy and valuable.

Self-image is how you regard yourself. It is the mental image you have of yourself and how others perceive you. Only then can you fully focus on your goals, desires and dreams without distractions from the ghosts of your past or a beaten down self-image within and succeed.

Unfortunately, some people focus attention on their weaknesses and major in their minors or what they cannot do or lack skills in. By this they debilitate themselves and run their gifts, skills and abilities to ground. To succeed, major in your strengths. Focus on the things that are working in your life and make the most of them. What is your mission or purpose in life? Find it and focus all your time and effort on it. What is it you want to be remembered for? This is the time to work at it with laser sharp focus and gain knowledge, skills, proficiency to succeed in it, being recognised and acclaimed.

Successful people focus on their legacies and work on them daily. For instance, Richard Branson said his legacy is, "He lived his life to the full and didn't waste a moment of his time." He uses every working moment to work towards that.

Also Steve Jobs was noted and recognised at Apple for technology. Michael Jordan is famed for Basketball. Henry Mancini is remembered for music and film scores. Arthur Ashe is memorable for tennis. Charles Dickens is still remembered for his memorable verses and books about London life. What is your natural talent and area of accomplishment? Focus on your gifts, abilities and talents. That's why you've got them. Develop and sharpen them. Gain knowledge, acquire skills to help you direct and focus them to where they can help you succeed and become the best you can.

Successful people choose to do what they love most. This helps them to focus on it with concentration, commitment, passion and energy. It also motivates them to keep doing it for longer. For example, Serena Williams likes winning tennis grand slams and collecting trophies. Steven Spielberg loves making movies, Warren Buffett loves investing money and Tiger Woods loves playing golf. Oprah Winfrey loves doing Television documentaries. Doing what they love most helps them avoid boredom and to commit to excellence in their field.

They also update themselves continually with learning new things to creatively add more value to their business. They are successful and exceedingly wealthy and happy.

When you invest time, energy and effort doing what you do best, the things you are brilliant at and love to do most, people will beat down the door to congratulate and crown your effort with deserving success. Then wealth will automatically flow to you.

Setting boundaries

Are you a homemaker or a home business owner? Are you a student or scholar? Are you a wage worker or wonder worker? Whatever your personal or professional life is, you need to set boundaries for your success. If you don't, others will pull you every which way, but Success Street. They will distract, divert and disturb to derail you.

If your time is important to invest in your success, you must protect yourself from distractions and diversions from time wasters, telephone marketers and gossips. Perhaps they have no desire to succeed at anything. Why should they derail you from your goals and desire to succeed?

Set boundaries and enforce them with no excuses and no exceptions. Friends and family are the worst offenders if you have not briefed them on how important your time is. But when they know, they'll support you and help to protect your time from other time wasters.

Learn to say No

There are many calls on our lives in this technological age of information overload. But successful people learn to say no without feeling guilty or ashamed. The biggest challenge some people have in focusing their attention is that they get dragged away to one event after another because they just cannot say no. If people understand where you can and cannot go, they will often respect your time and your wishes.

You don't need to oblige every acquaintance or friend with your time to remain friendly with them. When you have succeeded, you will find successful friends who truly understand the real value of time and how best to use it for more success.

Some may try to push the boundaries but if you stick to the plans, none can divert your attention from your designed route to success, namely focusing on what you do best that on achievement, will aid your success. We all have the same 24/7 hours, learn to use and manage yours wisely and effectively as all successful people do.

Exercise to chapter 5

Part A

- List five activities that you can do to increase your productivity or earning ability by 10%
- List them again in order of importance and priority
- Select the one activity that will have the greatest impact on both productivity and your earning ability
- Focus all your energy, attention, time and resources on this one activity until you have completed it.

Part B

- What is your greatest natural talent?
- What is it that only you can do so well that others marvel?
- Can you build a product or service around it with cash opportunities?

If so get creative, concentrate on developing this talent until its brilliance shines.

Part C

- What is your worst bad habit that distracts you from major work?
- Can you give it up, delegate it or outsource it?

Set yourself effective boundaries to guard your most valuable resource – Your time

CHAPTER 6

Passion

Nothing great in the world has ever been accomplished without passion

Georg Wilhelm Friedrich Hegel

Passion is a deep feeling, an emotion or great enthusiasm. Our lives run on feelings and are driven by emotion. Feelings give form to thought, ideas and dreams. Without feeling they cannot take wings and soar in our imagination. With feelings they take form and crystallise as tangible substances. As Charles Haanel said, "The emotions must be called upon to give feeling to the thought so it will take form."

When you feel good about yourself, you give out good positive energy and attract the same form of energy to feel even better. However, when you feel bad about yourself or your situation, the reverse happens and you attract the negative energy you give out. Consequently, if you feel good about success, you will attract the positive energy, emotions, people, circumstances and events to help you succeed.

But If you feel bad and negative about success, money, relationships, your business or your career, no amount of goal-setting or affirmations will make you successful in those areas because your negative bad feelings already negate your success in that area.

As Neville Goddard said, "Be careful of your moods and feelings for there is an unbroken connection between your feelings and your visible world." Thus, your present circumstance is a reflection of your inner feelings in any area. When you change your feelings, you can change your outer world, circumstance and your life.

The importance of passion as a key to success lies in you feeling consistently good, positive and optimistic, expecting good things to happen. Even if the unexpected, unpredictable and uncontrollable thing happens, accept the inevitable and let your mind remain optimistic, energetic and enthusiastic about what is still working in your life. This draws positive energy to enable you reason calmly, clearly, see alternative opportunities and empower you to make the right decisions and avoid pitfalls.

Secondly, when you are always positive, passionate and enthusiastic in your actions and endeavours, you attract the same positive energy you give out. This empowers you to achieve your goals and succeed. As Ralph Waldo Emerson said, "Enthusiasm is one of the most powerful engines of success. Nothing great was ever achieved without enthusiasm." Passion is the fuel for success. Passion is also the power for your mission. It galvanises and empowers you into action to realise your dreams and propels to position you for success. It can turn your desires and dreams into reality.

Thirdly, passion or feeling is a great motivating force in our lives. We want success, more money or good nurturing relationships because they make us feel good about ourselves. We detest failing and pain that make us feel bad or sad about ourselves. Thus, if you can feel it, you can have it. Good positive feelings attract good things and bad negative feelings attract bad things. As Neville Goddard said, "A change of feeling is a change of destiny."

Today, make your desires and dreams for success in any area real and tangible, by passionately assuming the corresponding good feeling of having succeeded and watch the Universe move on your behalf to make it so. In other words, assume the feeling of having achieved your dreams. Live it now and see it manifest as your reality in very little time.

Exercise to chapter 6

List five ways to motivate yourself to remain positive and enthusiastic

- What areas do you want to succeed in?
- How do you feel about succeeding in those areas?
- Can you assume a feeling of having achieved your objective now?
- To accomplish great things you need great passion. How can you be more passionate and enthusiastic about your success in order to achieve it?

CHAPTER 7

Hard Work

The ascent of Everest was not the work of one day, nor even of those few unforgettable weeks in which we climbed…. It is in fact a tale of sustained and tenacious endeavour by many, over a long period of time

Sir James Hunt

Successful people learn early on the road to success that they can only succeed through hard, painful, gruelling work. If they endure the temporary discomfort and pain they would eventually win and enjoy long-term benefits. As Mohammad Ali said, "I hated every minute of training, but I said, "Don't quit. Suffer now and live the rest of your life as a champion." Everyone has the will to win and succeed. However, it is only the 5% who are willing to put in the time and effort continuously and consistently to prepare, practice and do what it takes to win that make it to the success finish line.

Hard work tends to separate people and turn on the spotlight on their character. As Sam Ewing said, "Some turn up their sleeves, some turn up their noses and some don't turn up at all." Unfortunately, without putting in the hard work at the beginning you cannot succeed. There are skills to learn, talent to sharpen, abilities to hone and knowledge to acquire before you can adequately lay a firm foundation for success.

For example, the unemployed people Jack picked up at the Job Centre in chapter 2. They shied away from work and never got to make any money. This confirms what Thomas Edison said, "The reason a lot of people do not recognise opportunity is because it usually goes around wearing overalls looking like hard work." But there is no substitute for hard work, if you are dreaming of success in any area of your life.

Take action

Hard work also means taking action. No matter how much you desire a thing and how big your dreams are without action, nothing will happen. Abraham Lincoln said, "Things may come to those who wait but only the things left by those who hustle." No matter what you know or what you think about the past, present or future, they are inconsequential without you taking action and hustling to bring it about. For instance,

Testimony

A young sixteen your old Malawian boy desired education. He dreamed of bettering himself. He said, "We have three million people in Malawi and twenty two graduates. Nobody has ever earned a degree from an American college. I want to be the first." These are lofty dreams for a young man whose parents were so poor that when he was born, his young inexperienced mother threw him into the river because she could not manage him and did not know what to do with him. But someone rescued him. He grew up and was later sent to the local school to learn to read and write.

Later he took action. He didn't just dream about being educated in America, he took the next step to make it happen. He had no money and no means of getting there but his burning desire became an obsession. He gathered the little he could and left home, barefoot and penniless, in search of education to better his life. Why?

He said, "In Malawi, young men grow up with no schooling, no work and they become thieves and damage the country. I want to do better." On the 14 October 1958, Legson Kayira left Nyasaland (Now Malawi) with a small axe, a world map, the bible, John Bunyan's Pilgrim's Progress and enough food for five days. He walked first to Kampala in Uganda, reaching there fifteen months later in January 1960.

This was the first leg of his long trek to glory or death. He worked to get enough money to feed himself before continuing on his journey. Somehow he managed to reach Khartoum in Sudan, a total of 2500 miles! He already secured admission and a scholarship to Skagit Valley College, University of Washington in Seattle. In 1965 he published a story of his long trek to glory, titled "I will try." It became a best seller and has encouraged others to take action to make their dreams and desires happen.

Today, what are you doing to make your big dreams and desires happen? As Robert Schuller said, "When you dream big dreams you tend to attract other big dreamers."

But you must first take action to get noticed by other big dreamers before they can help you. Legson Kayira, moved from his homeland on foot, to get help. In Kampala he saw an advert for a scholarship in America. He applied and was accepted. Had he not moved from his home, he would never have seen the advert and never would have gotten to America and become educated. You must take action to succeed.

Similarly, Frederick Douglass, was an American slave. He hated slavery and wanted freedom. He said, "I prayed for twenty years but received no answer until I prayed with my legs." When he took action to escape from his slave master, God answered his prayers. He risked being shot dead or captured and hung to set an example for others thinking of escaping. He took his life in his hands and ran for it. Despite the hardship along the way, he made it to safety and became a famous writer and orator.

Many complain and blame

Unfortunately, many people have big dreams and want to succeed, but can't attract other big dreamers because they spend their time complaining and blaming others. The parents you complain about and blame for your circumstances gave you birth and cared for you. What, have you done to honour and reward them in gratitude? Oprah Winfrey said, "It does not matter how you came into the world, what matters, is that you are here." What are you doing to better your situation and improve your circumstances? Legson Kayira said, "I learned I was not, as most Africans believed, the victim of my circumstances but the master of them." Are you a master or a victim of your situation? Victim mentality makes and keeps you a victim until you change it.

The relatives you complain about have allowed you to survive till now. Others died in infancy or childhood but you are still alive so what are you doing for yourself? The government you blame and complain about has provided the infrastructure for your success. How have you used it to improve your life? The God you blame for all your woes has kept you alive and sustained you till now, how grateful are you to Him?

Both Legson Kayira and Frederick Douglass took action to improve their plight and circumstances. They changed their situation before they attracted the help of others. They raised themselves out of abject poverty and ignominy and attracted world attention. Legson Kayira proved that it is possible to change the conditions of your birth. He did Africa, the nation of Malawi and his family proud. You can do the same.

What are you doing today to change the conditions of your birth? Only you can change your situation. Others may help you but until you take action, you will remain where you are still complaining and blaming others. You may hope, desire or dream like the man who sat in his rocking chair, wishing, hoping and praying for God to bless him with wealth and riches. He died, still rocking because he took no action to make it happen and bring his desires to pass. Today, decide to take action, be active and see what happens.

Be proactive to make things happen

Successful people are proactive. They make things happen by seeking opportunities for action. Unsuccessful people on the other hand, are reactive. They wait for things to happen or opportunities to show up before deciding whether or not to get involved.

Unsuccessful people therefore tend to see opportunities as problems to overcome while successful people are grateful for them, seeing them as challenges for action. Hence successful people often seize opportunity with both hands and get to work.

Testimony

For example, in 1980, while travelling with his wife, Richard Branson was stranded when a local Puerto Rican flight was cancelled. He did not check into the local hotel or start demanding that the airline give him a refund for his inconvenience. No. He thought of how to use the opportunity and make a profit. Because there were no other flights out that day, he phoned a few aircraft charter companies and chartered a private plane. Knowing that many people were stranded and needed to catch a flight badly, he quickly borrowed a blackboard and wrote "Virgin Airways $39, Single Flight to Puerto Rico." Within an hour of walking into the airport terminal and realising that the flight was cancelled, he managed to secure an alternative flight for the stranded passengers. He sold every seat within the hour. He successfully flew everyone back to Puerto Rico and made a cool profit for himself. This is being proactive. His idea later gave birth to Virgin Atlantic! However, opposite of proactive is procrastination.

Procrastination

This is the greatest obstacle to success in any area of life. Procrastination has been called the thief of time and the thief of life for time is life. It is a deadly negative habit. Andrew Carnegie, the man who gave the world the philosophy of success, called it "The antithesis to success habits and one of the worst of all human traits."

Procrastination is defined as the habit of waiting for just the right time before initiating action. It starts off as a choice to avoid unpleasant tasks until it becomes a habit for all tasks. It is to failure, what initiative is to success. It can be due to feeling negative towards task accomplishment. There are four main causes of procrastination.

- Lack of a definite, clear goal
- Lack of initiative
- Lack of self-discipline
- Lack of decision-making skills

Whatever the cause, King Solomon said, "He who forever waits for ideal conditions will never get his work done," (Ecclesiastes 11:4). Most people who indulge in this destructive negative habit just cannot get going. They lack the will to begin anything. They habitually frame reasons and form excuses why they procrastinate. It is an ingrained habit they are not willing to relinquish. Many are perfectionists, paralysed by analysis of minute details of each activity but fail to seize the big opportunity.

Those who aspire to succeed in life, take a sword to procrastination. They know that they must first conquer it before they can succeed. It kills motivation, drains energy and robs one of the opportunities for productivity and progress. It ensures failure. Thus, those who seriously consider success learn to discipline themselves to initiate action in the direction of their goals to negate procrastination. For without the self-discipline to form success habits, the initiative to take action and make things happen and the willingness to expend the energy needed, nothing can be achieved and the success you seek will become an illusion. Without success you cannot reveal your greatness.

But you can conquer procrastination.

Here's how:
- Take responsibility for your actions and inactions
- Own it as a bad negative habit to be conquered
- Manage your time better by getting rid of distractions
- Chunk your tasks down to bite sizes
- Write down your goals and visualise them daily
- List the consequences of not starting
- Overcome the fear of failing or of succeeding

Many people blame the wind, government, lack of help from friends and every conceivable thing for their inaction. Research suggests that procrastinators just have bad negative habits. The sooner they own up to it and decide to take a sword to it, they overcome and are free. Therefore own up and take responsibility.

Then chunk down your clearly written down goals to manageable sizes for you. There is something about written down goals that energise them towards fulfilment. If you visualise these goals daily you can will yourself to take action to achieve them. Ask yourself how important your goals are? Are they burning desires or just wishes? The obsession with which you regard your goals will determine the importance you place on their achievement. The less desirable they are the less you'll attempt them.

Effective time management is essential for success. Those disciplined to use time more effectively will succeed while those who don't, won't succeed. Action takes care of fear of failure and defeat. So get started on your task for the consequence of entertaining procrastination is failure. But the result of taking action is success.

Hard work can be fun

However, it is not all work. It can be fun if you do what you love and are passionate about it. Hard work becomes fun and ceases to be dull gruelling work. As Confucius said, "Choose a job you love and you will never have to work a day in your life." For instance, Serena Williams love winning tennis grand slams and Michael Jordan loves playing basketball. Thomas Fuller said, "All things are difficult before they are easy." Over time, the hard work ends and you begin to enjoy the fruits of your hard earned labour.

But if you want to achieve greater success, you must work harder. As Booker T. Washington said, "Nothing ever comes to one that is worth having, except as a result of hard work."

So be hard on yourself on your way to success and life will be easy on you.

Hard work is also the price you pay for your success. Nature demands her fair price and you must pay it in advance. Michelangelo said, "If people knew how hard I had to work to gain my mastery, it wouldn't seem wonderful at all." Four gruelling years of lying on his back painting the ceiling of the Sistine Chapel took its toll on him. With plaster and debris constantly falling into his eyes and making them sore and him not letting up on the work even to wash and change his clothes, paid off in the immortal legacy he left behind —a monumental achievement and successful accomplishment.

All successful people enjoy hard work so much that they are absolutely enthusiastic about it. For example, Thomas Edison said, "There is no substitute for hard work." Henry Ford of Ford motors' fame said, "There is joy in work. There is no happiness except in the realisation that we have accomplished something." To accomplish is to work hard at something worthwhile, blurring the line between work and fun until you enjoy it so much that it ceases to be tiresome, tedious work but fun and play.

Peter Drucker, wrote "Plans are only good intentions unless they immediately degenerate into hard work." Bill Gates still works eighteen hours a day in spite of being a wealthy billionaire and so does Brian Tracy. If these successful people can put in the hours for hard work, why can't you? There you have it, success demands hard work that gets easier over time. But you can make it fun by doing what you love with passion enthusiasm and positive energy.

Exercise to chapter 7

- Do you shun hard work because it is tedious?
- Do you miss great opportunities because they look like work?
- Do you get easily bored with work?
- Are you among those who hate their jobs but want promotion and a raise?
- How hungry are you for success?
- Have you conquered procrastination?
- What are your plans for turning hard work into fun and play?

Note: Many people become great and successful by doing what other people refuse to do.

CHAPTER 8

Go the Extra Mile

It's never crowded along the extra mile

Wayne Dyer

Going the extra mile means over-delivering on your promises. It means doing more than you are paid to do. It means giving more value to those who least expect it. By these actions many make themselves noticed by those who can help to lift them up higher or reward them. Some are transformed by their generosity and kindness and become more confident, more self-reliant and more influential to those around them.

For example, when T. Harv Eker started selling his exercise equipment, he would go the extra mile for his customers to set up the equipment for them and even teach them how to use it properly. This endeared him to them so much that they referred him to many of their friends and relatives. Within two years, T. Harv Eker made his first million dollars and has not looked back since. There is reward on the extra mile.

As a wage worker, going the extra mile means taking on more responsibilities to help out. It means doing those menial jobs others shun and some neglect to do and filling in time by coming early and leaving late. By these actions, you secure your job. You will be the first to be hired and last to be fired. You will get noticed by management and rewarded with promotions, new projects, bonuses, extra benefit and even raises.

As a business person, to succeed you must deliver more than you promise and pleasantly shock and wow your customers. Always add something over and above their expected package. This way you gather loyal customers routing for you and promoting your service to others. Many hotels are fully booked through holidays and dry seasons because of their exceptional service and customer care. When you are willing to do more than you are paid to do, eventually you will be paid more to do what you currently do. This is the key to success through going the extra mile.

As an individual, going the extra mile means demanding more from your mind and body in thought, effort and time spent on your goals and dreams. Expending extra resources in pursuit of your goals and ultimate success is what will set you apart from the crowd and hands you the success you seek.

For example, Michael Jordan said, "I expect more from myself than anyone would expect from me! When my coach expects me to train 3 times a week, I would train 5 times. When my coach expects me to score 15 points for each game, I would score 36 points! That is why I am the best in the world." When you are hard on yourself, life gets easier on you.

Unfortunately, some wage workers and business people fail to even deliver what they promised let alone go the extra mile.

They wonder why they lose customers, new clients or their patronage. Some workers spend time complaining about hating their jobs, co-workers, organisation and wages but do nothing to change their situation. Meanwhile some business people are focused on their next big marketing launch or their Olympian ego. Consequently, neither group can succeed, but remain mediocre.

Zig Ziglar wrote, "There is no traffic jam on the extra mile." He discovered that 5% of people succeed to enjoy 95% of all the income and wealth available while 95% of the rest struggle to share the remaining 5% of the wealth and riches because they refuse to go the extra mile for success. The legendary Roger Bannister said, "The man who can drive himself further, once the effort gets painful, is the man who will win."

If you seek success, going the extra mile by doing more than is expected of you by your boss, organisation, clients and customers is the sure route to success, raises, promotions and more profits in the long-term. Remember that givers always gain more.

The Universe ensures that. You can always be nicer, happier and more enthusiastic. Even relationships must add value for mutual benefit and profits otherwise they fail.

When you go the extra mile to help others grow and develop, they can do the same for others and your circle of influence becomes more mature and more valuable. The effort and energy expended is richly rewarded by the improvement in circumstances and the impact on other people's lives over time. There is great reward in choosing to go the extra mile in every arena of human endeavour and associations.

Things can be done better, quicker, nicer or be made easier and more user-friendly. You must rise above the average 95% to achieve success. Your product or service must be above average to attract attention and continued patronage for success.

Thus, this key to success is one you hold in your hands. Use it and succeed. As Ralph Waldo Emerson said, "Build a better mousetrap and the world will beat a path to your door." You can start right now to apply the habit of going the extra mile by rendering more and better service than you currently do and ensure your success.

Exercise to chapter 8

- Do you have the opportunity to do more at work and on your job?
- What could you accomplish with just a little more effort?
- How elated would someone feel if you did more than they expect?
- How would your clients and customers feel if you provided a little more service, nicer, better, easier, quicker and more user-friendly?
- Can you improve your products or services with just 10% more value or more effort?
- How can your relationships and associations be improved to profit all those concerned?
- What personal initiatives do you have in place for going the extra mile to do more for others and achieve more success?

CHAPTER 9

Personal Development

We have an innate desire to endlessly learn, grow and develop. We want to become more than what we already are. Once we yield to this inclination for continuous and never-ending improvement, we lead a life of endless accomplishment and satisfaction

Chuck Gallozzi

Through kaizen, the Japanese have perfected the idea of continuous improvement. Everything can be improved by 10% or more. This has become a personal mantra for millions of successful people. They continuously learn to improve their personal and professional lives and then add more value to their business to gain competitive advantage by being better, nicer, quicker and creating easier to understand and more user-friendly products to keep them above the competition.

For example, Virgin Brand took thirty years to develop through continuous improvement before it became credible and synonymous with quality. Today, that quality is stamped on unrelated businesses around the world!

All great achievers are committed to continuous improvement if only to keep up with the rapid rate of change. For example, Apple is number one in most markets having managed to create future generation products that are more user-friendly.

Their products can also do more and are easier to use. All these attract users to flock to their shops to enjoy the novel experience. Similarly, Starbucks and Costa have taken the art of coffee drinking to a whole new level of experience and are reaping the benefits of their creative innovation.

What about Nike in sports and Virgin in acquiring failing companies and turning them around with known-brand know-how? Thus, personal development is the route to crafting successful businesses and organisations.

Success seekers can decide and dedicate to being continuous learners, growing incrementally as they progressively achieve their worthy goal or ideal and become successful. Only you can develop yourself. You know where you are and where you want to be in a set time. You know the skills, knowledge, talent and ability that you need.

Oliver Cromwell said, "He who stops being better, stops being good." Good is always the enemy of better and best. Those who rest on being just good enough are soon overtaken by the better and the best. They soon find themselves irrelevant and obsolete.

Which area of your life needs improvement? Decide today and commit to continuous never-ending improvement. If it can work for a nation like Japan and make them successful, why not for an individual like you? Learn something everyday for when you are through with learning, you are through with life. To earn more or succeed more, you must learn more. So acquire better skills and improve your earning ability.

Benjamin Franklin said, "If a man empties his purse into his head, no one can take it from him." The knowledge, skills and experience you acquire as resources are yours alone. You can lose wealth and riches but if you have the resources you can rebuild your losses.

Discontentment with the status quo is the seed of innovation and creativity. Without desire for continuous growth and personal development, ideas for creativity will not come. Thus, personal development births the ideas for creativity and innovation to do more.

Personal development enables you to form the habit of learning more to be more. With continuous self-improvement comes the discipline to manage and use your time more effectively to accomplish more. None can continuously improve without the aid of self-motivation. You learn early to motivate yourself to keep learning to grow and mature in many areas like effective communication before you can succeed.

Most importantly through personal development you forge a character worthy of success. Such a character will help you to bounce back from set-backs and breakthrough breakdowns, disappointments, discouragements or temporary defeats and failure.

Without these pre-requisites to success, your quest would be hollow and failure is sure. Thus, personal development is the route to being skilled in self-motivation, time management, self-preparedness with ideas for creativity, self-disciple, building effective communication, know-how and forging a worthy character for success.

All great successful men and women were great at continuous learning. They were great learners and greater teachers. For example, Thomas Edison, Albert Einstein, Benjamin Franklin, Ralph Waldo Emerson, Confucius and Carl Jung were learners.

It was Confucius who said, "If I am walking with two other men, each of them will serve as my teacher. I will pick out the good points of the one and imitate them and the bad points of the other and correct them in myself." They learnt from life and from their students. They learnt from experience and anywhere they could. That's what made them successful as old masters, teachers and gurus because they practiced continuous self-development. They never grew stale and irrelevant even today.

Jim Rohn was one of America's foremost philosophers. He taught many lessons on personal development that have stood the test of time. He said, "Become self-educated. Standard education can only get you standard level of success and make you standard." When I embraced self-education I learned more than the years of college education enabled me to accumulate and I became more than when I left college.

He also wrote that success, wealth and happiness can only correspond to our level of personal development. Whatever you have not acquired through self-development you cannot have on the outside. These were great lessons and as we applied them we improved and surprised ourselves. He told us to learn more through listening and observing others and to work harder on ourselves than on our work, job or mission.

From him I also learnt to read a book a week so that in ten years I would have read about 500 books and become an authority in any field of interest. What a great man. I am deeply indebted and profoundly grateful for his influence greatly enriched my life.

Brian Tracy is also big on personal development and the qualities of effective leadership. He said, "If you wish to achieve worthwhile things in your personal and career life, you must become a worthwhile person in your own self-development." How do you become a worthwhile person? - Through continuous and un-ending self-development.

He taught us to invest a percentage of our income in our own personal development in order to guarantee our future. He told us that you cannot earn more than you are prepared for on the inside. But through personal development you can control your earning ability.

These were great success lessons to learn and apply. They also enriched my life greatly. The rewards and benefits of self-development far outweigh the cost in time, effort and personal sacrifices.

Today, you can commit to a journey of continuous personal development. Learn all you can so you can grow, develop, mature and succeed and then you can earn all you can get.

The benefits of continuous personal development and learning are:

- Self-motivation to learn more
- Self-discipline through commitment
- Effective time management
- Better communication skills
- New ideas for creativity and innovation
- Personal preparedness to meet opportunities
- Forging a worthy character for success

Personal development in these areas will ensure that you gain a master key to your success and succeed. For success depends on opportunity meeting prior, proper preparation, without which there is sure to be failure.

Relaxation

In your personal development for success, you must also factor in time to relax and have fun. Without the balance of activity, relaxation and fun, you'll get tired easily and become discouraged and probably quit. Without times of solitude and relaxation with stillness and meditation, there will be no divine inspiration to draw on for creativity.

Some relax by walking or going on long cross country hikes. Some listen to music while others read or do handcraft or paint or write poetry to relax.

Plan for fun

William James writes, "Begin to be now what you will be hereafter." Don't wait until you've succeeded or are happier to enjoy your life and pamper yourself. Start now. On your way to Success Street, practice being happy and relaxed now.

Successful people through the ages found ways to relax and energise themselves physically and get mentally inspired by letting their imagination soar and roam.

As Albert Einstein said, "Imagination is everything. It is the preview of life's coming attractions." Thus, they were motivated to foresee life's future attractions and have fun doing more and accomplishing more. For instance, Albert Einstein played the violin to relax and Winston Churchill painted while Henry Mancini took to the ski slopes. These great men were not trying to become experts with their fun-filled activities but they relaxed while meditating on the challenges in their areas of competence.

Testimony

Albert Einstein said, "I want to know all God's thought." How else can you commune with the Divine except through soothing music? King David proved it and became the singer of songs in his Psalms. Einstein recorded the importance of solitude and music thus: "The intellect has little to do on the road to discovery. There comes a leap in consciousness, call it intuition or what you will and the solution comes to you and you don't know how or why."

Now we know that during his relaxation, playing the violin, he created the atmosphere for divine inspiration like Old

Testament prophets, Elisha, Samuel and King David, who relied on music to enable them prophesy.

Similarly, Henry Mancini relied on the physical activity of skiing to energise him to produce such enduring film scores and music still unmatched in history. Others like J. Paul Getty, Thomas Edison and Leonardo da Vinci practiced solitude to get ideas and inspiration for their great work. Albert Einstein said, "The monotony and solitude of a quiet life stimulates the creative mind." This is what made them geniuses.

Relaxation can do the same for you if you can choose the right mode for your temperament to commune with the Divine and get solutions to challenges and answers to your questions. You will astound yourself by the level of intuition and inspired superior intelligence relaxation and stillness can provide to aid your quest for success.

Exercise to chapter 9

- How prepared are you to meet your opportunity for success?
- What motivates you to continue learning?
- What plans do you have for continuous learning and personal development?
- Which areas do you need to develop to earn more or be more?
- Make a plan of how you will develop yourself and set it as a goal to achieve
- Plan also to relax. Relaxation can motive and inspire you with creative ideas.

Here's to your success and happiness as you develop and grow.

CHAPTER 10

Service

I never perfected an invention that I did not think about in terms of the service it might give others... I find out what the world needs, then I proceed to invent

Thomas A. Edison

Everything in creation serves a purpose. The sun, moon and stars serve as designed in their appointed function. The rain and the four seasons serve nature to regulate growth. Many successful people identified a need and crafted services or products to meet the need. Similarly, your success will depend on how well you serve to meet human need by providing a solution to make things easier, better, quicker or nicer.

Testimonies

Bill Gates saw a future market need for computer software even during his early years at IBM. Subsequently, he wanted to put a personal computer in every home to give people access to the fledging internet. His success made him a billionaire.

Sara Blakely wanted women to dress and look good. She used and liked tights without toes and the experience drove her to develop a variety of products called Spanx. She succeeded and today she is a multibillionaire.

Amancio Ortega of Milan wanted to save his mother further embarrassment from store keepers because she didn't have enough money to purchase groceries. He quit school and started working in the clothing industry. While other teenagers played ball, he opened his clothing stores. Today, he owns Zara stores and is a billionaire.

A housewife managed to conquer the mayhem in her home during mealtimes with her young family. She thought about other mothers suffering as she did so she wrote a book about it to help them. Today, Jo Turner is marketing her book titled "Meal times without mayhem," to help mothers with young families manage mealtimes without the attendant mayhem. She has succeeded and is making waves.

Henry Ford saw a need for transportation from horse drawn carts to the motor car and met that need. Later he said, "A business absolutely devoted to service will have only one worry about profits. They will be embarrassingly large." He succeeded.

The steel magnate Andrew Carnegie saw a need for steel during the American push from the East coast to the West coast. He was a day labourer at the time. He turned his desire to supply steel into action to meet the industrial need. His steel plants served to make railways, industrial machinery, buildings and motorcars possible and solved people's problems. It made him the richest man in his generation. He said, "Generally speaking, riches and material things that men get are the effect of some form of useful service they have rendered. My fortune did not come to me until I had delivered to others, definite value in the form of large quantities of well-made steel."

What in your experience constitutes a need with marketable value? How can you help others to reduce suffering, look good, feel healthier, make more money, learn more, lose weight and keep it off, find the love of their life or succeed in life? Need is everywhere. Just open your eyes and ears from the shopping malls to the markets, from the stores to stories people tell. People are seeking help and solutions for some ailment or something else.

As Carl Jung said, "Nobody as long as he moves about among the chaotic currents of life, is without trouble," or need. So find solutions to needs and prepare to serve humanity with answers to people's problems. For the success you seek, like wealth, is never attained when sought after directly. It comes as a by-product of useful service. Service also brings satisfaction and useful profits!

Why service? Henry Ford wrote, "The foundation of real business is service." Jim Rohn also said, "Whoever renders service to many puts himself in line for greatness - great wealth, great return, great satisfaction, great reputation and great joy." If for no other reason, build your business on useful service for great success.

Tennis players and entertainers provide great entertainment for the spectators and earn themselves bundles of money in the process.

Albert Einstein said, "Only a life lived for others, is a life worthwhile. The value of a man should be seen in what he gives and not in what he is able to receive." Your reward with success will always be in direct proportion to your service to others.

You may express your joy and satisfaction from service in a different way but first, you must succeed like these people and then glory in your successful service.

Exercise to chapter 10

- Ask yourself, "How can I be of useful service to other?"
- Some feel that the highest honour comes from service
- How can service bring you empowerment through helping others?
- In what areas do you currently serve?
- How do you plan to serve others and humanity, in future?

CHAPTER 11

Commit to Excellence

The will to win, the desire to succeed, the urge to reach your full potential…these are the keys that will unlock the door to personal excellence

Confucius

Excellence means high quality, distinguished, superior and of merit. It is being the best and doing the best that you can. Commitment means dedication and devotion. Success will not elude you if you are dedicated to high quality in service, products, relationship, work or association and committed to unrelenting pursuit of excellence.

It is very easy to become and remain mediocre. Just find a few friends doing nothing and going nowhere and associate with them for a season. Their influence will rub off on you and you'll soon become just like them. Never underestimate the power of influence, be it negative or positive. Choose your associates and friends with care.

If you also spend time with dream killers, they will drown everything and every idea you have with so much negativity, like a heavy wet blanket and make failure certain.

However, if you always focus on being the best and dedicate everything you do to that, the quality of your life will be in direct proportion to your level of commitment.

All successful people commit to being the best in their fields of endeavour. They aim for the moon and shoot the stars. As Steve Jobs said, "Say no to a thousand things." Then focus and commit to a few things where you can gain real mastery and excel.

By continuous leaning and relentless practice, you gain mastery, become excellent, proficient and succeed as the best. Commitment inculcates and instils self-discipline by doing.

Testimony

The legendary Zig Ziglar, told a story of how he mastered sales. As a young man he went into sales but he just couldn't sell anything. When his wife delivered their first child, he had no money and borrowed to pay the medical bills. After two long years as a salesman with nothing but zeros on his scorecard, he was thinking of quitting.

Then one day at a seminar, the speaker watched him and saw the fire of enthusiasm in his eyes and commented saying, "You know Zig, I bet by this time next year, you could be the number one salesman in this city." They both laughed. There were 7000 salesmen in that city. Zig could not see himself overtaking them having sold nothing so far. But he kept on with his rounds and doubled his efforts. He committed himself to making excellent presentations and attending all sales meetings to learn more. Within the year, Zig Ziglar started to make sales. He never compromised his attitude or excellent methods by cutting corners.

At the end of the year, Zig did not make it to the number one spot as the speaker envisaged. Zig was the number TWO salesman out of seven thousand sales people! What a brilliant performance from someone who committed to excellence to achieve his goal. He went from zero to hero in sales and earned himself millions of dollars in commissions. He also broadened his horizons.

Today, you too can commit to excellence in all areas of your life. Make it a habit and dedicate time, effort and resources to being number one in all things you undertake. You too can go from zero to hero or she-ro. Zig did it. Why not you? As Colin Powell said, "If you are going to achieve excellence in big things, you develop the habit in little matters. Excellence is not an exception or a skill, it is a prevailing attitude."

For instance, Michael Jordan has an attitude of being the best in basketball. He said, "I expect more from myself than anyone would expect from me! When my coach expects me to train 3 times a week, I would train 5 times. When my coach expects me to score 15 points for each game, I would score 36 points! That is why I am the best in the world." His attitude and commitment to excellence became a habit that paid off for him and can do the same for you in your field of endeavour.

Develop an attitude of excellence and succeed. Sports men and women know the power of committing to excellence that propels them to the pinnacle of their sports.

For example, Mario Andretti, the former racing driver said, "Desire is the key to motivation, but its determination and commitment to an unrelenting pursuit of your goal - a commitment to excellence- that will enable you to attain the success you seek." For him the goal became a commitment to excellence and he excelled.

When you commit to excellence, you've got to give it all you've got and more to make it happen. That's what makes you a winner. Commitment to excellence also earns you handsome rewards and profits. For instance, during the making of the film Star Wars, George Lucas wanted some special effects to set the film apart. He was told that it could not be done. He could have accepted the conventional wisdom and bowed to the experts.

However, his attitude and habit of committing to excellence took over. He formed a separate company, Industrial Light and Magic, to create the effects he wanted. Result, the film was a monumental success, grossed $290million and earned him $50million at the age of 28! Such is the reward of committing to excellence and saying no to average, ordinary existence that leads to mediocrity.

Tiger Woods also commits to being the best and staying at number one during his winning seasons. Mohammad Ali committed to being the champion and trained tirelessly. He motivated himself and built up mentally with positive attitude until he believed it and went on to become the enduring champion he is in boxing. Through commitment they all became more. Today, current sports people like Serena Williams and Rafael Nadal also commit to being at the top of their game to win matches. You can emulate their commitment and work on your dream to become more.

They developed enduring self-discipline, resolute self-confidence and the resolve to follow through and win no matter what. As Zig Ziglar said, "It was character that got us out of bed, commitment that moved us to action and discipline that enabled us to follow through," and succeed in winning and reaching our goals to live our dreams.

Self-discipline

Haile Gebrselassie writes, "Once you have committed, you need the discipline and hard work to get you there." Successful people are self-disciplined and hard workers. Discipline is defined as the ability to make yourself do what you should do whether you feel like it or not. We are all ruled by feelings and emotions. When we don't feel like it we generally don't do what we know to do. But to succeed in life you cannot afford to run your life on the whims of emotion hence the need for self-discipline.

Your commitment to excellence strengthens your resolve and helps to break the power of inertia and resignation to mediocrity in your life. It enables you to do what you should do in order to succeed, come rain or high water, whether you feel like it or not. Successful people develop such an incredible level of self-discipline that makes any procrastination from taking action or losing focus from their goals and objective almost impossible. That's what makes and keeps them successful.

Successful people, by self-discipline, take immediate action. Once their imagination births an idea, they speedily take action and run to market with the ideas and gain momentum. Thus, by self-discipline they've learned to dare to move with ideas to market at lightning speed and gain first-mover advantage to massive profitability.

When discipline inculcates and instils habit in your daily life, it brings order to a chaotic lifestyle. When you discipline yourself to do what you must do to succeed, life will not discipline you and you would avoid the pain of regret, disappointments and missed or lost opportunities.

Discipline drives you towards goal achievement. Without the daily discipline to take actions that move you towards your desire and dream, you may never get there. Therefore discipline yourself and order your life aright so you take action to succeed.

Habits

Discipline also builds habits. Our lives are ruled by habits. They make life run on autopilot so we do what we should from habit and not conscious thought and feeling. To build habit takes consistent and repeated action over time. This allows new neural pathways to widen and deepen in the brain like a new footpath in the forest.

By repetition, the surrounding "thorns and thistles" are cleared leaving only a wide footpath to traverse. The old underused pathways are overtaken by "weeds" and cease to exist after a while. Consequently, the consistent repetition of actions, help to build success habits that eventually will birth the desired success. As Bertrand Russell, the philosopher said, "Right discipline consist, not in external compulsion, but in the habits of the mind which lead spontaneously to desirable rather than undesirable activities." Thus, self-discipline leads to doing the desirable acts that can bring you success and avoiding undesirable pain of regret and disappointment from inaction.

Successful people are reputed as being dependable and reliable through living disciplined lives of doing what is right and doing it right as routine without thought.

Meanwhile unsuccessful people procrastinate and complain, lose focus on their goals and become distracted by minor challenges and unavoidable natural events.

"Discipline is also the bridge between goals and accomplishment" said Jim Rohn. Without the training of discipline most goals cannot be accomplished and achieved.

The New Year's resolution is a case in point. People make them in earnest but without the self-discipline needed to follow through to completion their desires are soon dashed and derailed by old habits of self-indulgence, forgetfulness or inaction. Thus, success is the accumulation of success habits developed through disciplined activities repeated over time.

How else can Michael Jordan consistently remain the world's number one? Discipline; How can you succeed in your quest? Discipline; George Washington said, "Discipline procures success to the weak." Celine Dion confirmed it by saying, "There has been nothing but discipline, discipline, discipline all my life." Result? She achieved mega success in Vegas and around the world to feed her lifestyle.

Vidal Sassoon disciplined hair

Even ladies' hair had to be disciplined to form the habit of falling back into shape and performing as expected to help ladies look and feel their best in order to succeed personally and professionally. When you look good, you feel good and give your best. For instance, Vidal Sassoon said, "We learned to put discipline in the haircuts by using actual geometry, actual architectural shapes and bone structure. The cut had to be perfect and layered beautifully, so that when a woman shook it, it just fell back in." If the king of hair succeeded in his career by disciplining ladies' hairstyle, why can't you discipline yourself to do what it takes to succeed in your life?

Physical Health Discipline

Many people complain that they have big bones and therefore cannot control their weight. Some claim that it is genetic. Whatever the reasons, self-discipline is the route to physical health and fitness. For instance, Brother Kenneth Copeland used to be overweight. He did not pray for God to reduced his weight and make him slimmer. He prayed for wisdom to know what to do. He realised that his diet was faulty. He said, "I don't eat slices of bread I eat a loaf." Well, eating a loaf of bread for breakfast had adverse effects on his weight and health. When he cut out bread from his diet, he lost a lot of weight and has kept it off. He did not ask God to zap his weight and reduce it through a miracle. He did it by himself.

Similarly, seek the wisdom and self-control through discipline to understand what foods make you put on excessive weight.

Success in other areas would be meaningless to you if you cannot live to enjoy it. Many cannot climb up a flight of stairs without breathlessly panting for an hour. Self-discipline is the route to better eating habits, fitness through regular exercise and avoiding health hazards. With discipline in your health, you can live out your days with joy and contentment.

Bo Bennet writes, "The discipline you learn and character you build from setting and achieving a goal can be more valuable than the achievement of the goal itself." The essence of success strategies is to refine you and expand your consciousness as a more valuable person in readiness for the lifestyle of success you desire. Therefore, a character suitable for such a lifestyle must also be developed through discipline.

Character

Helen Keller writes, "Character cannot be developed in ease and quiet. Only through experience of trial and suffering can the soul be strengthened, ambition inspired, and success achieved." The suffering and pain of self-discipline to build character, is the price you pay for your desired success. For without first succeeding on the inside, you cannot attract success on the outside. You become what you are within.

Character is having the resolve and backbone to do what is right because it is right and then doing it right. It is being the same in private and public no matter what it costs you. It is keeping your word of promise at all cost. It is saying what you mean and meaning what you say without ambiguity. It is having integrity and a reputation for honesty. Integrity means to successfully integrate, align and combine all your strengths and weaknesses into a functioning whole.

It means being the same from all sides. Reputation is the estimation or value others attach to you, your name and your word. A person of character is whole in private and public, highly esteemed and trusted by others. He lives a life of respect and integrity whatever his career, status, educational standard, position or job. Theodore Roosevelt said, "I care not what others think of what I do, but I care very much about what I think of what I do! That is character." Character gives you that personal power that grants you respect from others.

This is gained by keeping and meeting your obligations as contracted with others.

Character is forged from disciplined habits. As Stephen Covey said, "Our character is basically a composite of our habits. Because they are consistent, unconscious patterns, they constantly, daily, express our character." Thus, character is a habit of daily choosing between right and wrong, moral and immoral, work and play, valuable and worthless. Through daily choice, we decide and take consistent action to build a worthy character that stands the test of time by honouring our obligations. Success demands it. Without such character, the scandals of Enron and World.com will repeat themselves and commitment to excellence would be meaningless and unprofitable.

A true test of character is in doing what you must do whether you feel tired, stressed out, discouraged, disappointed or dissatisfied, no matter how much you dislike the action.

Character is what makes people trust you and want to do business with you or give you credit. It is what attracts the best to you because you are committed to being and are progressively becoming the best. It is the basis of success and excellence.

Without self-discipline and character, enduring success, in any area, will be elusive. Therefore, commit to excellence and build a reputable character and self-discipline in preparation for a lifetime of success. When opportunity comes you will not be found wanting, look unprepared or foolish. Without this prior preparation you can't succeed.

Warren Buffett said, "It takes twenty years to build a reputation and five minutes to ruin it. If you think about that, you will do things differently." When you painfully forge your character in the furnace of self-discipline, on the crucible of building success habits, your reputation will automatically take care of itself. Why?

Because the moral and ethical standards you choose to uphold will be upheld whatever the situation or circumstances. You will not easily be bought at any price and your values will remain intact. For instance, Joe Lieberman was a United States Senator from Connecticut. He was also the Presidential running mate of Al Gore for the 2000 elections. Joe is an orthodox Jew, who values his Sabbath on Saturdays. During the Presidential campaigns, Joe would not campaign on Saturdays. Not even the lure of the US Presidency could force him to change his values and campaign. Everyone accepted that and respected him for his faith. Fast forward during the Trump Presidency, Joe would still not attend any events billed on the Sabbath. That is character and living by your integrity.

In a world of unethical behaviour and dishonest practices, those who live by integrity, seldom compromise their values on any issues. They meet their obligations. Thus, build your character on your values and honour them, come what may.

Aim to live a life of integrity and character forged through self-discipline to support your successful life. As Og Mandino said, "The discipline of character provides the power with which a person may ride the emergencies of life instead of being overwhelmed by them."

Exercise to chapter 11

- In what ways are you committed to excellence?
- List the areas you aim to excel
- What plans have you in place to help you excel in these areas?
- Do you aspire to be excellent?
- Are you committed to excellence?
- Why commit to excellence?
- Are you a person of integrity?
- Do you live by honouring your word?
- List five ways you can show yourself as a person of integrity, who lives by his or her word of honour.
- Success is measured by your level of self-discipline, so how disciplined are you?
- If you are not disciplined how do you plan to include discipline in your plan of actions to achieve success?

CHAPTER 12

Perseverance

Never give up on your dreams… Perseverance is all important. If you don't have the desire and belief in yourself to keep trying after you've been told you should quit, you'll never make it

Tawni O'Dell

Perseverance is defined as dogged determination to carry on. It is the resolve to keep making effort despite difficulties. It is the tenacity to endure all and reach your goal. It is the ability to withstand and weather challenges without losing enthusiasm or faith in yourself until you win. It is a key of success and an attribute of champions. But this determination to persevere will be tried and tested by all until proven as real.

Rejections

Successful people go through countless humiliating rejections in their endeavours before they make it. But they don't let rejections faze them. For example, Colonel Harlan Saunders is reputed to having had 300 rejections for his Southern Fried

Chicken with special recipe before someone gave him a break. He was retired and over 65 at the time. Today, his KFC restaurants are on most major streets of the world. That's tenacity and dogged determination to reject rejections and finally win.

Zig Ziglar said he specialised in rejections during his salesmanship days. If they rejected him or his products he just brushed it off and went to the next prospect. In the end he succeeded. Today, where are those who rejected him and his products?

Many people are not meant to buy from you, relate to you or be nice to you. The sooner you understand the dynamics of human behaviour and buying habits, you will cease to be discouraged or frustrated by rejections. Then the fear of rejection that robs some people of self-confidence and the courage to go out and have fun will finally flee.

Many authors battle with rejections from major publishing houses. This gave birth to self-publishing and alternative modes of publishing better suited to the electronic age we live in. Thus, rejection can become a source of creative innovation.

For Instance, author John Creasey holds the world record for rejections. He collected 743 of them from publishers before he sold his first book. He went on to become a successful author of 562 books in his time. If he was not daunted by rejections, why should you? As Sylvester Stallone said, "I take rejection as someone blowing a bugle in my ear to wake me up and get going, rather than retreat." Thus, rejection can become a spur for more action or adjustment of tactics to overcome the challenge, not an affront.

Overcome CRAP

Apart from the obvious and most debilitating negative emotion, that devastates many people namely, lack of acceptance or rejection, there are other negative attitudes people display. These I call CRAP (criticism, condemnation, refusal, abuse and pressure).

To succeed in life you must devise a way to overcome and counter them with either positive attitude or emotions. They are facts of daily living and dealing with them is important for your success. Otherwise they will discourage you, force you to regard yourself as worthless, inconsequential, less than and become insecure. They can also drown your self-esteem and the self-confidence to pursue and attain your goals.

Awareness and resolute determination NOT to make other people's opinion, words or actions become your reality is mandatory to overcoming CRAP. You will get them from the grocery store to government bureaucracy, from peer pressure of bullies to executive ruthlessness of the powerful. Every human social interaction involves CRAP.

The worst crap happens in service industries. Those who serve must take the CRAP. It is part of the deal. If you detest taking the CRAP, then keep away from service firms. Most people bear their heavy burden of life and wish to share them with others. If they are angry they unleash their anger on others. If they have been abused, they tend to abuse others. If they are suffering, they'll ensure others share their pain and sorrow and suffer. As W. Somerset Maugham said, "It is not true that suffering ennobles the character, suffering for the most part makes men petty and vindictive."

For example, during my research into hotel services at different hospitals I was amazed at the level of crap dished out to the support service workers. Obviously, some patients are in pain and discomfort. However, some patients also want others to feel their pain. They verbally abused the service workers and called them names. They often threw rubbish on the floor deliberately and rang the bell for someone to come and clear it up. Some complained about loss of money and personal possessions that were later found to be untrue.

Meanwhile they accused the workers of theft! The service workers were most gracious and humoured them. They knew that they were there to serve and keep their jobs so they maintained a happy grateful attitude and took it all as part of the service. It was a revealing experience. Thus, to succeed, you must commiserate often, sympathise and cajole always but avoid these unfortunate people in their dream world of negativity and move on with your life and work.

Fears and Past Failings

There are also fears and failings that can dog success seekers. You must learn to put the past behind you daily and move on. Allowing yourself to ruminate and dwell on the past, what people said and did or did not say and do, will derail your success.

Instead use the lessons learned from any pain of your past to design and fuel better, much brighter future for yourself. There is no better revenge than massive success. Henry Ford said, "What is past is useful only as it suggests ways and means for progress. There is no disgrace in honest failure; there is disgrace in fearing to fail."

Michael Jordan said, "I have failed over and over and over again in my life, and that is why I succeed." To succeed, you keep failing until you stumble on success.

Successful people determine early to forego their past as a luxury and focus on their future. You cannot move forward with clarity unto your desired destination always glancing at the rear-view mirror. You will either crash or abort the mission and go live with the cold ashes of your past. Success is a matter of daily choices and priority. Choose wisely, let go of your past and focus on your goals as successful people do.

Jealousy and Envy

There is jealous envy from family members, relatives and self-professed enemies. Alexander Pope said, "If a man's character is to be abused, there's nobody like a relative to do the business." Many people just don't like to be overtaken by others. They are happy when you are all in the same barrel just crawling about like crabs and getting nowhere. The moment they see or hear you trying to succeed and move on, they fear abandonment. Furs will fly and fangs and claws will tear to wound as bitter hatred and anger rear up their ugly head to vent venomous, critical and condemning words on you. Why?

As Aeschulus wrote, "It is in the character of very few men to honour without envy, a friend who has prospered." Jealous envy is as natural to man as breathing. But jealousy can be a spur for some people. However, bitter envy is a deadly foe.

Therefore be prepared to duck and move on. You cannot focus on your goals for success and take them on. Decide to let them be and let go of rebuttals, explanation or excuses for wanting success. It's your life. Furthermore, Carter Godwin Woodson said, "Men of lesser magnetism grow jealous when others make inroads in areas they think they are more competent." People will always be jealous of others doing better than they are. In your pursuit of success, beware of the fangs of jealous envy.

Success killers

Some success seekers suffer from their own inability to deal with personal success killers. These are comfort and complacency of doing what you've always done and getting the result you've always got without much success. They refuse to change.

Secondly, some resort to blaming others when the inevitable challenges come or complain about their lack of knowledge and skills to function. They refuse to acquire what they seem to lack or update themselves and continuously develop to improve.

Thirdly, some follow the path of least resistance by doing what is easiest and least taxing. By tackling minor challenges, your level of success will remain minor or at best mediocre. When you deal with major challenges that can most impact your goal and success you will succeed in a major way and the minor challenges will be taken care of. Those who tackle and deal with more taxing challenges eventually become more valuable so they succeed more and earn more. Success through perseverance is rife with choices, priorities and adopting a winning positive attitude. Success is also won and attained through persistence.

Persistence

> Patience, persistence and perspiration make an unbeatable combination for success

> Napoleon Hill

Persistence is the determination to carry on. It is endurance without tiredness. It is grit and a firm resolve to see a project to the end. Successful people acknowledge that the road to success is through persistence and patience while sweating it out in hard work. Through the ages it has not changed. If it were easier and less arduous, everyone will be a success and not the present 5% of the population.

But those who stick to their set goals and objectives like the humble postage stamp until they arrive at their desired destination will succeed. For example, tennis ace player, Bjorn Borg said, "My greatest point is persistence. I never give up in a match. However down I am I fight until the last ball. My list of matches shows that I have turned a great many so-called irretrievable defeats into victories." It worked and made him a legend in tennis. Why not for you?

Personal Testimony

Similarly during my research studies, almost everything seemed to work against me but through sheer persistence, I complete my thesis and went through without rewrites. The power of persistence to aid success is measured by its results. We have proven it through self-discipline of consistently taking action and commitment to the course. As Calvin Coolidge said,

> "Nothing in the world can take the place of persistence.
> Talent will not; nothing is more common than unsuccessful men with talent. Genius will not; unrewarded genius is almost a proverb.
> Education will not; the world is full of educated derelicts.
> Persistence and determination are omnipotent.
> The slogan "Press on" has solved and always will solve the problem of the human race."

Unfortunately, many success seekers quit when they are close to victory. The pain and pressure of discouragement, defeats, and disappointment take their tolls and they quit. As Ross Perot observed, "Most people give up just when they're about to achieve success. They quit on the one-yard line. They give up at the last minute of the game, one foot from the winning touchdown." But the few people, who hang in there, resolutely determined and persist in doing the work no matter how unlikely success seems, will eventually succeed and win. That's the power of persistence.

Exercise to chapter 12

- How persistent are you in pursuing your goals?
- Do you give up when the going gets tough?
- Persistence is a decision and not a skill, so how do you decide?
- Do you persevere through challenges and obstacles until you win or do you give up?
- Do you resign to the comfort of doing only the usual in conformity of what worked for you in the past or do you find new ways of doing things?

CHAPTER 13

Maintain a Positive Mental Attitude

The greatest revolution of our generation is the discovery that human beings, by changing the inner attitudes of their minds, can change the outer aspects of their lives

William James

Your circumstances reflect your inner state. Whatever you are within, you manifest by attracting similar circumstances, people and events on the outside. This is the law of attraction simplified. For example, if you are a bitter and angry person, you will exude bitterness and anger as your dominant aura and this will magnetise and draw to you, negative circumstances, people and events in line with your angry bitter state of mind.

However, if you adopt a more positive attitude of passion, enthusiasm and excitement to life, you will also attract positive emotions, circumstances, events and people into your life to help you win and succeed in your endeavours.

Positive attitude is a state of thinking, feeling and acting in a positive and favourable way despite contrary events, trials and daily troubles. Positive minded people are full of enthusiasm, passion and energy in everything they do. They are not easily fazed, distressed or daunted by setbacks, disappointments and discouraging events. They don't allow negative people or events to adversely depress them with criticism, rejection, gossip or angry outbursts. They manage setbacks and failings well and accept them as stepping stones and set up for greater comeback. They can easily break through the barriers of distress and depression. These attributes and attitude enable them to succeed in their daily endeavours.

Most successful people maintain a positive winning attitude of champions because attitude determines their level of success and ability to get what they want. They know that positive mental attitude accounts for 80% of success in any arena of life.

Complete the past

However, to develop and maintain a positive winning mental attitude of successful people you must first complete your past and be liberated from all that threaten to limit and hold you back from the success you seek. Negative habits and self-limiting belief must he laid to rest and unsupportive mental conditioning dealt with before you can develop positive mental attitude. John Stuart Mill said, "No great improvement of mankind is possible until a great change takes place in the fundamental constitution of their mode of thought."

In other words you must change your thinking and attitude before there can be any visible change in your outward condition or circumstances.

This is because you cannot develop anything positive and empowering on the sewer of your negative, distorted and contrary thinking or be filled with positive energising emotions while harbouring toxic, de-motivating and self-sabotaging negative ones. So what are these negative emotions and self-limiting beliefs to be laid to rest?

Colin Powell said, "None of us can change our yesterdays but all of us can change our tomorrows." You cannot change what happened to you in the past. No matter how much and how often you rehash, replay and relive them, those past events will remain dead like cold ashes in your imagination. The only reality you have is now.

Unfortunately, many people bear the Herculean burden of their past and log them along through life. Some still revisit what their dead parents and elders did or did not do forty years ago! They claim that those actions or inaction limited and kept them bound from success and progress for forty years and they could not make peace with themselves. Unfortunately, while they play the blame game and condemn their parents, life moves on and they miss out on living.

Whatever childhood events, negative words or actions that you think limited you, you must resolve them for the sake of your sanity and future success. Your parents, foes, relatives and friends, dead or alive, did the best they knew how and could do in the circumstances. Surely forty years is enough time to correct a wrong, counter their limiting effects and move on. Until you change your thinking about a situation nothing in your life, regarding that situation will change.

James Allen said, "Most men are anxious to improve their circumstances, but are unwilling to improve themselves; they therefore remain bound" to negativity, resentment and anger from events of their past.

Also any negative conditioning based on words you heard or events you witnessed and gave meaning to, you must find a way to change them. These may have led to limiting beliefs about money, people, relationships or demeaning words about you that dented your self-esteem and drowned your self-confidence. Even if those people meant to harm you but you survived till now, shouldn't you let go and move on?

No amount of validation of your story by others can change the circumstances or events. So let go of the past. Regard it as completed and done. All dues paid and move on. Until you do, success in any area of life will only be a mirage for you.

You are made or unmade by your daily choices to let go and be free or be bound to the past.

Bitterness

Nelson Mandela said, "Resentment is like drinking poison and then hoping that it will kill your enemies." Bitterness from any cause grows deep in the psyche of those who harbour it. Like the sycamore tree used for caskets and coffins, when fully grown it produces fruits of anger, hatred, jealousy, sarcasm, revenge and spiteful cynicism that can defile all around.

Unabated bitterness becomes a mental stronghold that grips and kills its possessor because of the gall and wormwood that afflicts to poison major organs like the liver.

Often some people can see a valid reason for harbouring these deadly emotions. They rationalise and defend them from an offended victim's standpoint. They base their whole life on what was done to them which they can never forgive or forget and seek revenge at all cost. Unknown to them, the offending party is often unaware of the offence and lives life oblivious of their negative consuming emotion. Meanwhile the gall of bitterness corrodes to destroy their joints and damages their internal organs.

Until you lay down your anger and bitter resentment, no matter the cause or cost and forgive those who harmed, limited, took advantage of, abused and misused and conned you, you may as well forget success. These negative emotions are incompatible with success.

Forgiveness

Marianne Williamson writes, "Our past is a story existing only in our minds. Look, analyse, understand and forgive. Then as quickly as possible, chuck it away." The more you analyse, relive and replay the past, the more you will find hurts, wounds and scars from your past. Your mind will play tricks on you reminding you of what words were intended to mean and how hurting and wounding those words were. It will do this and blame it on the devil. Forgiveness is your route to peace of mind and freedom from the past.

However, if you choose to let go of all the junk of the past and reframe unintended harsh words to reflect your current standing and dreams, their negative connotations will disappear and you will soon laugh at the foolishness of remembering them. How do I know this? I chose a long time ago to live by what I call the law of contentment.

Personal Story

During my three years in my own wilderness finding myself, I came across the writings of Sun Tzu, in the Art of War. I learnt so much from his writing that I adopted some of his verses and made them my own. For example here are six of his best:

1. When I let go of what I am, I become what I might be
2. When you are content to be simply yourself and don't compare or compete, everybody will respect you.
3. Mastering others is strength. Mastering yourself is true power
4. Silence is a source of great strength
5. Be content with what you have; rejoice in the way things are. When you realise there is nothing lacking, the whole world belongs to you.
6. To fight to conquer in all our battles is not supreme excellence; supreme excellence consists in breaking the enemy's resistance without fighting

During my solitude to find myself, I read these words over and over until I made them my own. Today, I still practice the law of contentment. It states that "When you are content with the way things are, the whole world belongs to you." Furthermore, you can win the war against enemies by breaking their resistance through unconditional love and forgiveness. No one can fight you if you refuse to engage in combat. When you forgive, you move on. If others choose to be bitter and angry at you that's like water off a duck's back.

It merely washes and runs off you without harm. You live at peace with contentment. When you let go of anger, hatred and bitterness, you can succeed and manifest your greatness. Why sacrifice your destiny on the altar of minor skirmishes with negative misguided and purposeless people going nowhere and having no dreams in life?

This policy enriched my life and helped me to let go of all the past hurts and wounds and develop a positive attitude of contentment through whatever life throws at me from any quarter. You too can let go of your past and develop a positive mental attitude today.

Avoid negative people

Jim Rohn writes, "You are the average of the five people you spend the most time with." Never underestimate the power of influence. Whoever you choose to run with, you would imitate and model your life on theirs. If they are predominantly negative, your outlook will become negative until you change your friends and associates.

As Apostle Paul said, "Do not be deceived, evil company corrupts good habits" (1 Corinthians 15:33). "But as iron sharpens iron, so a man sharpens the countenance and habits of his friend," says King Solomon (Proverbs 27:17).

Therefore choose people who can lift you up and encourage you to be more than you are now. One of the reasons for choosing positive like-minded people with big dreams and passion to live their dream is that they understand your challenges and aspirations. But dream killers don't understand why you want to succeed. They feel you just want out from their group and go solo. They think you want to abandon them because now they are not as cool and up to speed as your new found success. You can love them from afar but you must leave them if you want to succeed and live your dreams.

Negative people think, feel and act negative. They are oblivious of their situation and attitude. As Les Brown said, "You can't see yourself in the picture when you are in the frame." They don't see themselves as negative, contrary, critical, blaming and complaining about everything and everyone. If you allow them to keep you in the barrel, like crabs crawling about, they will keep clawing you down to their level and there you will remain. Later in life when it is too late, you will regret and rebuke yourself.

As Wyland said, "There are two types of people— anchors and motors. You want to lose the anchors and get with the motors because the motors are going somewhere and they're having fun. The anchors will just drag you down." Run with successful people and learn their success habits. Avoid negative people and stay positive.

Successful people refuse to even deal with negativity and those who harbour them. Why? They realise that negativity from any source breaks their focus on their goals. It drowns their courage, enthusiasm and optimism to get through disappointments or failings. It drains them of much needed energy and saps their physical strength for hard work.

Since hard work is the route to success, no successful person has time for negative people or their negativity. However, if they choose to change, they will be received, accepted and accommodated. Otherwise their ugly attitude will not be entertained or tolerated. Emulate successful people. Avoid negativity and negative people without exception.

Negativity is both contagious and highly infectious. It can spread through a home, department or an organisation like a plague, infecting and afflicting everyone in its wake. One negative person can contaminate and demoralise a community in no time. Before the contagion is contained, productivity grinds to a halt and profit is history.

They can derail individuals and organisations by keeping them busy with needless arguments or putting out the fire of conflict, broken promises and attitude they bring. Therefore, avoid negativity and negative people like the plague and blight they are.

Similarly, avoid the daily news, media and magazines that bombard us with negative ideas, doom, gloom and endless sensational drama. These destructive negative ideas feed the mind with counter intentions and drive you on the downward spiral to abort your deepest dreams and desires of success.

On the other hand, when you fill your mind with new, positive ideas through reading positive books, and listening to positive motivating material, they will inspire you with feelings of excitement, passion, enthusiasm and laughter.

These emotions attract positive energy to help you win. Today, choose to fill your mind and life with positive energising thoughts and ideas.

Develop a Positive Attitude

Before you can develop a positive winning attitude of success like the champions of success, you must ensure that you have a foundation of a healthy self-esteem and the emotional balance to handle success. This is reflected in your level of confidence and the courage to dare and succeed. Success assumes emotional balance.

Successful people have a healthy self-esteem. They value, respect, absolutely love and appreciate all that they are as worthwhile, happy and valuable people. They take total responsibility for their lives and don't blame anyone for their plight or position. They don't wish to be anyone else because they are happy being whom they are.

As Brian Tracy said, "The happiest people in the world are those who feel absolutely terrific about themselves and this is the natural outgrowth of accepting total responsibility for every part of their life." They truly love themselves and have positive attitudes. Thus, they have a foundation of healthy self-esteem, on which to build their courage and confidence and go out and dare to succeed. They also maintain their success because they are mentally and emotionally prepared to handle every aspect of it.

Personal Story

As a young child I was very shy. My parents' love and affection gave me a very stable foundation on which to build a healthy self-esteem. However, I was still shy and very reserved. I loved my books more than going out and meeting strangers. After I qualified as a medical doctor, I was still shy and hid my shyness behind the consultation table. My confidence was only based on my professional status.

As an adult I needed to find myself and find meaning to my life outside the medical profession which I regarded as a career. The opportunity came during my transition from medical practice to teaching. I went away to discover what to teach and in the process I discovered myself. By this I mean that during my three years sabbatical, I read every book that I could find on most subjects like emotional intelligence, communication, interpersonal skills, positive mental attitude, success principles, psychology, effective leadership, personal development, spiritual meaning of money, education, teaching, biographies of famous and successful people, histories of nations and books by the old masters like the art of war by Sun Tzu. As I read them, a whole new world opened up for me. My vocabulary increased outside medical terms and I grew in knowledge.

At the same time I was reading the Bible to find meaning to my calling and mission. For two years, I listened to every preacher and speaker that had anything worthwhile to say about the Word. Between my reading and listening, the Word came alive to me and in me. I discovered the meaning I was searching for and this boosted my healthy self-esteem to another level. My confidence also grew to a higher level.

In the final year, I became more selective on what I listened to and used it to augment my learning and build faith. Thus, the Word gave meaning to my being, calling and mission. It defined and framed my life with purpose while my now enlightened belief gave me an identity in Christ.

My studies in personal development and general reading in all other subjects also augmented my subsequent education to heighten my level of confidence and gave me a voice outside medical practice. I was now prepared, mentally and emotionally to tackle any subject matter without self-doubt.

Consequently, my inner being and my outer doing became congruent or aligned to my calling to teach. I have a healthy self-esteem and an identity based on my relationship with Christ and an academic voice through achievements in my doing. I could now handle success in any form. Thus, my wilderness experience transformed me from a shy medic to a self-assured, confident individual and gave me a voice with which to speak and teach others.

You may not find yourself or the core of your being, through a wilderness experience. You may already have a self-assured consciousness of who you are. However, the totality of your being is what gives you a healthy balanced self-esteem as a basis on which to develop and build your self-confidence through successes in your doing. These will align you to handle success in any arena of life and maintain it.

Some people succeed in sport, commerce or education before they build up the core of their being. Either way you need both the being and doing to handle your success. Without a stable assurance of the person you are, a healthy self-esteem and confidence to withstand the vagaries of daily life and the critics, you cannot handle success or remain positive.

For example, the National Lottery jackpot winning by some bus drivers dubbed, the Corby syndicate is a case in point. Since the winning, most of them have either left Britain or Corby because they couldn't handle the emotional fallout from their sudden financial gain. One of them, John Noakes, said, "Sometimes I wish I'd never won."

According to Camelot, the organisers of the Lottery, "The transition from being broke to rich can be tough and winning can be an overwhelming emotional experience." Thus, those who are not mentally, emotionally and psychologically prepared for any form of success often cannot handle the social and emotional fallout from it.

Today, build and boost your self-esteem, the foundation on which confidence and success are built. Appreciate and treasure all the small daily winnings that constitute your actions from being and doing. When combined, these will ensure your success and keep you positive.

Examples of Prepared Minds

Nelson Mandela had a dream to rescue his native land from the injustice and racial segregation called apartheid. It took him through thirty years of poverty and being resented by others and twenty seven years of being incarcerated in the notorious Robben Island prison. He was a political prisoner but he never lost hope. Even when things looked bleak and hopeless he remained hopeful. Instead of wallowing in discouragement, despair and depression, he used the time to prepare himself physically, emotionally, psychologically, mentally and spiritually for the expected victory and success.

Consequently, the cold concrete prison floor could not freeze him out, disease and depression could not douse him out, prison warders could not weed him out or shout down his dreams and when the appointed time of his idea and dreams came, no power on earth could stop it. He rose from his degradation as a victor and was crowned with success.

Martin Luther King junior had his dream of a racially united America and announced it to the world in 1963. Many sceptics laughed and mocked him and his wild dreams. When the appointed time came, a young African American, self-prepared and ready, rose up and was handed the ticket to the White House.

President Barack Obama became the first African-American man to rise to the post of a president. Again it took struggles and forty five years to happen but it came to pass and today we are living that dream. As Victor Hugo said, "All the forces in the world are not as powerful as an idea whose time has come." These men were positive and hopeful, never wavered in their faith.

Viktor Frankl was incarcerated at the notorious Auschwitz, Dachau and other concentration camps during World War 11.

He spent three years there. Many prisoners died around him. Some died of despair, disease or were gassed in the chambers. But Viktor survived. Why? He maintained a positive hopeful attitude.

He wrote, "When we are no longer able to change a situation, we are challenged to change ourselves." He could not change the war, being a prisoner or the conditions he found himself in but he could change himself. He chose to be hopeful and not descend into gloomy despair, discouragement or depression that could have spelt death to him. He said, "Everything can be taken from a man or woman but one thing: the last of human freedoms to choose one's attitude in any set of circumstances, to choose one's own way."

He chose to prepare and preserve himself with a positive mental attitude. He chose his own way, the way of victory despite setbacks, bleak prospects and hardships. He chose life instead of death even though people were dying all around him like flies. He chose to succeed in his dream to leave Auschwitz alive and tell his story, rebuild his life and live his dreams. He lost everything but his optimism, hope and undying faith in his faithful God of justice and equity.

Today, be inspired by these great men of dreams and visions. They saw hope and a better life. They dreamed and held on, no matter the bleak and barren challenges they faced. In the end they realised their dreams and succeeded.

Today, you can succeed with your dreams and aspirations. You can develop the positive optimistic attitude they did that enabled them to say no to discouragement, defeat and despair. You can choose to stay positive and live to achieve success.

Staying Positive

Wade Boggs writes, "A positive attitude causes a chain reaction of positive thoughts, events and outcomes. It is a catalyst and it sparks extraordinary results." Ordinary people can accomplish extraordinary things simply by choosing to stay positive in every given situation. You have no control over people, their caustic and toxic words, negative actions, events, circumstances or the weather. But you can control your response to them. As Viktor Frankl said, "Everything can be taken from a man or woman but one thing: the last of human freedoms to choose one's attitude in any given set of circumstances." Positive attitude is a choice. Today, you can choose it.

For example, if the weather changes, you can change your clothes. If people turn sour and become abusive and demeaning you can vote with your feet and exit their presence. If events turn contrary to expectations, review your plans, find alternatives or cut your losses and move on. I have noticed that some contrary events eventually turn out for my benefit. I may have to wait awhile to see things turn around but they often do and I am so glad they were contrary at first. The joy of an unexpected favour!

Why Stay Positive?

- Positive attitude keeps you free from depression and discouragement

- Positive attitude lifts your spirit and lets it soar beyond your dire bleak surroundings and circumstances
- Positive attitude is like rain falling on dry caked soil, cooling and soothing to soften it
- Positive attitude motivates you with passion to take action to reach your goals
- It liberates you from negative self-talk that criticise and condemn you for we have what we say.
- Positive attitude boosts your confidence and energises you to go out and win
- It magnetises like-minded people, events and situations to help you win
- Positive attitude draws positive energy into your life to live a happier, healthier life of joy and fun
- It counters the negative energises of self-doubt and self-sabotage and empowers you to shatter both and gain your freedom from fear.
- Positive attitude attracts like-minded people to you for better nurturing and fulfilling relationships you desire and deserve.

Positive mental attitude is really the master key to success. No matter how best you apply all the other keys, without a positive mental attitude you cannot harmoniously attract the people, events or favourable circumstances to help you succeed. Without these favourable events and people as opportunity, all your prior preparation will be waiting a long time for the success you envisage. Why? Let the master of financial success explain.

Andrew Carnegie said, "A man may have all the culture modern civilisation can provide and he may have a string of degrees after his name a yard long and he may be the most skilled man in the field, but he will be a failure as surely as two and two make four, if he carries a bad mental attitude around with him! The one thing people simply will not tolerate is a negative mental attitude."

Negative attitude is worst in experts. Some carry around a bloated Olympian ego that blights their excellent work. Most people will settle for less skill with a pleasing personality than tolerate an expert with an egotistical, overbearing negative attitude. Be warned.

Negative attitude is a potent repellent of people, events and favourable circumstance and opportunities. It attracts the worst of events and people. It brings out the worst in people and ruffles their feathers. It often offends and descends into bitter resentment and anger. Nothing good was ever achieved with a negative mental attitude. Thus, today choose this supreme success key. Decide to master and maintain a positive mental attitude.

Physical Health

But of course your positive attitude for success must also include success in your physical health. As someone recently said, "Having all the success and money in the world isn't much good if you can hardly get out of bed in the morning to enjoy it!" So take good care of your health. Physical and mental fitness are crucial for success.

Thomas Edison said, "The chief function of the body is to carry the brain around." A fit body and fit mind complement each other. Therefore feed your body well with nutrients, minerals and vitamins. Exercise it to keep it fit and in optimum condition. Exercise has the added advantage of producing endorphins, the feel good factor, to keep and maintain your positive attitude. It also energises your body for hard work.

Feed your mind with relevant new knowledge to keep it active and functional. This would ward off any risk of dementia or Alzheimer's in later years. With energy, a fit body and mind, longevity and sanity will grace your successful years like a garland.

What can positive attitude do for your success?

- ✓ Positive attitude is the surest way to success through self-development struggles while having an exciting time of your life
- ✓ It is a proven way to personal power, prestige and prosperity through success
- ✓ It is the quickest way to settle any disputes and quarrels through supreme excellence of non-engagement in verbal combat but practicing unconditional love, acceptance and forgiveness
- ✓ It is the main way to manage conflicts by going the extra mile to be nicer, more friendly and more tolerant hence disarming any combatants
- ✓ Positive attitude is the safest way to serenity and peace of mind by practicing the law of contentment
- ✓ It is the roadway to riches, respectability and reputation by building a worthy and noble character and living a life of integrity in line with the success you desire.

- ✓ Positive attitude is the right way to right the things that can go wrong by choosing to lay down all resentment, anger and bitterness from the events of the past.
- ✓ It is the pathway to productivity and promotions by going the extra mile to do more and so become more
- ✓ It is the open door to opulence and abundance through an attitude of gratitude and contentment in the way things are while pursuing your goals
- ✓ Positive attitude is the catalyst for creative innovation by inspiring new ideas and self-motivation to action
- ✓ It is the door to your dreams and desires being realised and having more fun
- ✓ It is the highway to enduring health, wealth, happiness and longevity
- ✓ It is the perfect way to a pleasing personality that attracts support from others
- ✓ Positive attitude is the gateway to getting what you want in life - success

Exercise to chapter 13

- How positively minded are you?
- What is your dominant attitude to life and challenges?
- Do you stay strong or wilt in the face of opposition?
- Attitude is a choice, which have you chosen – positive or negative or the in-between?
- The benefits and rewards of a positive attitude are many. How attractive and alluring are they to you?
- How committed are you to success? For without a positive mental attitude, real success is not possible.

CHAPTER 14

Gratitude and Forgiveness

The value of a great idea lies in the using of it

Thomas Edison

The journey of success and the strategies or steps that can guide anyone to achieve it have been discussed. This final chapter is the icing on the cake, the baker's dozen or the difference maker on the route to success. Many who applied them succeeded much faster and easier than those who failed to apply them. I call them the power duo of success.

Gratitude

Gratitude is a quality of being thankful and a readiness to show appreciation for mercy, grace and kindness received. This feeling of thankfulness and the mental attitude of being appreciative separates the sheep from the goat, or the really successful from the mediocre.

As Wallace Wattles said, "The mental attitude of gratitude draws the mind into closer touch with the source from which the blessings come." On the other hand, most people who may otherwise order their lives aright are kept poor and impoverished by their lack of gratitude. Thus, gratitude for grace received opens the door for more grace or blessings.

For example, the Lord Jesus gave thanks to God the Father for hearing His prayers and honouring His words. This connected Him with the source of power for His miracles. How much more then should we give thanks in every situation and reap the rewarding blessings? Therefore an attitude of gratitude connects the grateful ones to the source of divine blessings and the power to act and get results. This is success.

But a mind set on discontentment and dissatisfaction with the way things are or a critical spirit with things as they are attracts and draws the poor, squalid and mean states of life and they will come to such a person. Remember the Israelites in the wilderness. They were dissatisfied with the promises and miracles of God and were never grateful for them. They never reached the Promised Land. They all died untimely in the howling dry desert.

The power of gratitude lies in the fact that all things, like events, circumstances and people have contributed to bring you to where you are today. You survived abuse, misuse and conflicts where others perished. Therefore as you give thanks for them, providence continues to protect, shield and guide you into your desired haven in your journey of success.

Personal Story

I taught Bible class to several groups of ethnic minority women from diverse areas. They came from West Africa, Malaysia and Singapore, some from West Indies and the Caribbean and some from East Africa. They were emotionally traumatised and wounded by their experience, at the hands of mates, relatives and co-workers. Some were abused, misused, abandoned and rejected by those they trusted to protect them. They were angry and wanted revenge.

However, as we studied the Bible together, they realised that revenge was not an option. So they started to give thanks for their survival. As we prayed together and gave thanks daily, they started to heal from their emotional wounds and smile again.

We continued on our journey of daily reflection and their recovery and their anger started to wane. But the pain within them remained and we needed to get rid of the pain and let go of the past so they could move on. We added forgiveness to our recovery steps.

Forgiveness

As stated before, forgiveness is for our benefit and not for the abuser or offender. It does not condone the violence or abuse we suffered but it wipes the slate of the past clean so we could move on with our lives. As they forgave their tormentors and abusers, their healing process accelerated and many of them healed. Eventually they let go of all the hurt and anger of the past in order to rebuild their lives. They all left joyful with new found confidence and courage to face the outer world.

Those who were on the dole gave up their social security allowances to try and earn their own living. Some were promoted to managerial posts with increased pay and allowance. Those who were indebted, had their debts cancelled or paid off, freeing them from economic hardship. Thus they all succeeded in completing their past in order to rebuild their future.

Success is a journey and not a destination. Those who by choice travel on it and obey the simple but powerful laws of success will succeed in their quest. Those who disregard these laws will not. Some people through conformity to the way things are and comfort in what has worked for them in the past, remain where they are and fail to succeed. To experience something different, you must think and act differently. As James Allen said, "Man is made and unmade by himself. By the right choices he ascends. As a being of power and intelligence, he holds the key to every situation."

Success is learnable and doable. No one was born successful. To succeed you must start from where you are, with what you have and diligently and patiently apply these success strategies with perseverance. The time it takes to succeed is immaterial since you are having an exciting fun-filled time of your life with enthusiasm, passion and energy along the way. The zeal of a two year old is to enjoy the journey or the ride.

Success is transferable. The same strategies, tools and techniques that worked in one area can be used to succeed in other areas. Successful people don't aim to succeed once or in one area. No. They use lessons learned in one area and apply them in other areas of their business or life. Richard Branson's

Virgin is a potent example of multiple unrelated businesses flourishing under one brand name. This is leverage. The ability to use skills and abilities learned elsewhere to gain competitive advantage in other areas and multiply your profits.

Those who give wings to their dreams through imagination to envision a better and more glorious future can manifest their greatness through success. Those who focus on reaching their dreams without distraction, diversion and desirable alternatives can reach their desired destination and succeed. But those who allow themselves to be diverted and distracted by distraction, negativity or broken focus with alternatives, will fail.

Those who dream big will achieve bigger, more important things than small cautious dreamers. Those who can emotionalise their dreams by assuming the feeling of having achieved their desires will succeed faster. Feeling is the ultimate answer.

Those who do what they love will find that hard work becomes more fun and less like work. Those who work for wages merely to meet their needs will take longer to succeed because they are not in alignment with their dreams, mission in life and their mental attitude to work. To them money and work are only a means of existence and survival.

Those who go the extra mile by doing more than is expected of them will find more promotions, prestige and rewards for their effort. Doing more is the price of success. As James Allen said, "He who would accomplish little must sacrifice little. He who would achieve much must sacrifice much. He who would attain highly must sacrifice greatly."

But those who concern themselves only with doing what they are paid to do will continue to be paid to do without succeeding in any particular area of their lives. They are the eternal wage workers, focused on the present or immediate gratification at the expense of their future greatness and glory.

Successful people learn to defer immediate gratification to focus on future multiple gains. Therefore, they invest most of their earnings and live on the rest, while most unsuccessful people spend most of their earnings and save a little for a rainy day.

Those who undertake the route of self-development will continue to grow to mature and remain fresh and current, inspired by new ideas for creativity and innovation. Their dreams and desires will be aligned with their beliefs and habits to direct their actions and attitude towards achieving their goals to attain the success they seek. They will also learn the self-discipline necessary to develop and build a worthy character and live with integrity. These are pre-requisites for a successful life.

Those who serve will be rewarded with benefits and profits. The whole essence of business enterprise is service. When you do better than others, without comparing yourself with them, you gain the edge and competitive advantage for better rewards.

Those who commit to excellence and have a clear sense of direction, travel easier and more joyfully on the journey of success. They also persevere better through all the inevitable bouts of failure, discouragement and disappointments along the way. The strength of your commitment to hard work and excellence determines the level of your persistence through challenges and rewards or profits from diligent service.

Those who cut out all that holds them back from success, like bad eating habits, or self-indulgence, will succeed while those who continue to indulge themselves won't. Your success is a measure of your level of self-discipline in all areas of your life.

Those who let go of their past through unconditional acceptance of where they find themselves without blame and complaints but with total responsibility to making the most of their lives, can succeed and live their dreams. Those who still wallow in the sewer of anger and resentment because of the uncontrollable events of their past will remain bound, mired in resentment and grow bitter and sour like the sycamore tree, fit only for caskets and coffins. Positive mental attitude is a choice we can all make.

If self-development is a major key to success, positive mental attitude is the master key for without it no success is possible. As Thomas Jefferson said, "Nothing can stop the man with the right mental attitude from achieving his goal: nothing on earth can help the man with the wrong mental attitude." There you have it. Choose a positive mental attitude of champions. It has been tried, tested and approved through the ages, from Presidents, pastors and peasant to enlightened gurus, engineers and entrepreneurs. They all applied these keys of success and crowned their effort with a positive mental attitude to reap the rewards of this master success principle and key.

Today, is your mind positively attuned to the success you desire? As Andrew Carnegie said, "People get that which their minds dwell upon; and this applies to a group or community or a nation of people, the same as to an individual." Whatever your mind consistently and constantly dwells upon—success or failure, is what you will eventually achieve. This is a proven law of success as it is a universal law.

All great and noble men and women who make life pay on their terms through success do so by obeying these success laws and giving orders to their creative minds through possessing and maintaining a positive mental attitude.

Today, you can join their ranks and succeed. Success is only a route to reveal and manifest the glory and greatness within you. Dare to succeed and you will. Let the world see and experience your true greatness and the glory upon your life. That's what it means to attain success.

Final Words

To laugh often and much;

To win the respect of intelligent people and the affection of children;

To earn the appreciation of honest critics and endure the betrayal of false friends;

To appreciate beauty and to find the best in others;

To leave the world a bit better, whether by a healthy child, a garden patch or a redeemed social condition;

To know even one life has breathed easier because you have lived.

This is to have succeeded

Ralph Waldo Emerson

These 12 simple strategies that guide men and women to success have been set forth and discussed at length. But no amount of reading and studying them can make you successful without their patient and diligent application. Therefore, to attain the joy of success you seek, apply them to your daily life. For as the wealthy, wise and successful Andrew Carnegie said, "Those who live by these principles as a matter of daily habit will profit by them in contrast to others who neglect to apply these principles."

Dr. M. Joshua-Amadi

Further reading
Man's search for Meaning by Viktor E. Frankl
The Psychology of winning by Dr. Denis Waitley
Then Darkness Fled by Stephen Mansfield
The Wisdom of Andrew Carnegie by Napoleon Hill

Also by Dr. M. Joshua-Amadi:
The Confidence to Live your Dream
The Joys of Life -Selected Poems

About the Author

Dr. Mabel Joshua-Amadi is a retired medical doctor, philosopher and an ordained minister.

She is the founder and director of a registered charity helping those disadvantaged by circumstances or customs to heal from their emotional wounds and regain self-reliance and reconnect with family and to become productive members of their community and society. Many people have achieved this goal. Further details of her charity work, writings and articles can be found at: www.libertyinternational.org.uk

After retiring from medical practice she started writing poetry and continued during the Covid-19 pandemic. She has since published the first volume of her selected poems, The Joys of Life.

Dr. Joshua-Amadi used these strategies discussed in this book to educate herself from nothing more than divine grace. She succeeded and attained several degrees along the way. Apart from her medical and post-graduate medical degrees, she holds an MBA and a doctorate degree from the University of Westminster, London. She is a student of practical philosophy and enjoys reading widely and learning new things.

Dr. M. Joshua-Amadi

126